Legacy:
Thoro Harris Gospel Music's Composer™

PUBLISHED BY LIFE PRESS™

ALL RIGHTS RESERVED

1st PRINTING

Copyright © 2024

Bernie L. Wade, PhD

Table of Contents

Preface 2

Chapter 1 – A Child is Born 4

Chapter 2 – The Ark is Coming Up the Road 26

Chapter 3 – Apostolic Faith Leader 42

Chapter 4 – His Living Musical Legacy 59

Chapter 5 – All That Thrills my Soul 73

PREFACE

No song writer, composer and publisher has impacted the Gospel of Jesus Christ through music more than Thoro Harris. Thoro composed more than 1000 gospel songs, published song books for hundreds of organizations, denominations and groups including the Apostolic Faith Movement, the original Pentecostal Assemblies of the World, the Assemblies of God, the Church of the Nazarene, the Seventh-day Adventist (and other seventh day groups), and a plethora of holiness factions. Yet, when asked about Thoro Harris, it is met with; "Who"? In the pages of this book, we expect to give the reader a glimpse into the man who penned so many Gospel Songs and was a key influencer in the lives of so many ministers of the Gospel.

While it is Thomas Dorsey who is called *The Father of Gospel Music*; it is Thoro Harris that composed or inspired many of the Gospel songs and hymns sang by several generations.[1]

From an early beginning as a child prodigy, Thoro Harris became a prolific organist, hymn writer and minister. He worked closely with Gospel greats like **Bishop Garfield Thomas (G.T.) Haywood, Fred (F. F.) Bosworth, Aimie Simple McPherson, Charles Fox Parham** and so many others. He left a legacy of worship that we celebrate.

Bishop Bernie L. Wade, Sr.
Presiding Bishop International Circle of Faith (ICOF)
www.icof.net

---

[1] https://en.wikipedia.org/wiki/Thomas_A._Dorsey

Thoro Harris circa 1920

Chapter 1

A Child is Born

*Who can cheer the heart like Jesus,
By His presence all divine?
True and tender, pure and precious,
Oh, how blest to call Him mine!
All that thrills my soul is Jesus;
He is more than life to me;
And the fairest of ten thousand,
In my blessed Lord I see.*
—Thoro Harris

Thoro Harris came from an accomplished family of ministers, doctors, authors, politicians, abolitionists, composers, writers, etc. Amazing accomplishments for any family but even more so for one dealing with the excessive burden of racism, slavery, and the post slavery environment in the Reconstruction period after the American Civil War in United States.

Siblings Worthie Harris Holden, poet, and Thoro Harris, composer.

"The one-drop rule was a legal principle of racial classification that was prominent in the 20th-century United States. It asserted that any person with even one ancestor of African ancestry ("one drop" of "black blood") is considered black (Negro or colored in historical terms). It is an example of hypodescent, the automatic assignment of children of a mixed union between different socioeconomic or ethnic groups to the group with the lower status, regardless of proportion of ancestry in different groups. This concept became codified into the law of some U.S. states in the early 20th century. It was associated with the principle of "invisible blackness" that developed after the long history of racial interaction in the South, which had included the hardening of slavery as a racial caste system and later segregation. Before the rule was outlawed by the Supreme Court in the Loving v. Virginia decision of 1967, it was used to prevent interracial marriages and in general to deny rights and equal opportunities and uphold white supremacy."[2]

Thoro Harris was born on March 31, 1874, in Washington, DC. His older sister Worthie was born 3 years earlier on March 11,

---

[2] https://en.wikipedia.org/wiki/One-drop_rule

1871, in South Carolina. The children were born to what was then called a "mixed race" couple, Dr. Joseph Dennis Harris and Elizabeth Worthington Harris. In a society that required nearly everyone to identify as either black or white (not counting Native Americans and those of Hispanic or Asian descent), Worthie and Thoro would eventually "pass" into white society. In contrast, their cousin Esther Georgia Irving Cooper,[3] identifying as black, became a civil rights activist, and their uncle, Cicero Richardson Harris, was a prominent bishop in the African Methodist Episcopal Zion Church.[4]

Bishop Harris

Worthie and Thoro's parents married in North Carolina at a time when interracial marriages were illegal, but the details of how they circumvented this law are missing. What is clear and makes this story so interesting is the insight it provides into the process of "passing." According to a 2019 study from the Bureau of Economic Research, passing was a widespread phenomenon in the United States between 1880 and 1940. In the Jim Crow era of oppressive discrimination, rigid segregation, and "one drop" policies that assigned race based on association, to successfully pass required active choice, dramatic changes, and secrecy akin to entering witness protection. It also required that one has enough European ancestry that one's physical features could pass for white.

Dr. J. D. Harris 1868

---

[3] https://en.wikipedia.org/wiki/Esther_Georgia_Irving_Cooper
[4] https://www.wikitree.com/wiki/Harris-40018

Paternal Heritage

Thoro's father, **Joseph Dennis (J. D.) Harris** was freeborn in 1833 the fifth child.[5] He was of "mixed race ancestry".[6] He was born into a household of mixed free and enslaved "colored" people around 1833 near Fayetteville, North Carolina. By 1840 it appears that Joseph's father, Jacob Harris, presided over a household of at least eighteen people: he and his wife, eight children, four apprentices, and four slaves. J. D. Harris was seven years old. The census for 1840 did not report individual names, apart from the head of household. We can identify the apprentices from indenture papers, but the slaves are known only by their ages—two males under ten, one female under ten, and one female between the ages of ten and twenty-three.[7] Jacob Harris was identified as apprentice master for eight apprentices in the 1830s; there were four teenage males in the household in the 1840 census.

What to make of the four slaves? As John Hope Franklin pointed out, free Blacks might own slaves for the same reasons that whites did—to advance their owners' economic well-being by the value of their labor, whether on farms or in workshops. Such owners can be identified, argued Franklin, by their extensive property holdings and their "inactivity in the manumission movement." For example, the famous Black cabinetmaker Thomas Day used slaves for thirty years to assist in furniture production; other free Blacks acquired agricultural land and put their slaves to work farming. But more common was the purchase of slaves for benevolent reasons. In families where one or more members were free,

---

[5] Humphreys, Margaret. Searching for Dr. Harris: The Life and Times of a Remarkable African American Physician. The University of North Carolina Press, 2024. Project MUSE. https://dx.doi.org/10.1353/book.124178.
[6] Virginia Humanities Encyclopedia. J. D. Harris (1833-1884).
[7] Ibid. Humphreys.

but others remained in slavery, it was common for the freed people to purchase relatives with the goal of ultimate liberation. Courts did not always allow such manumission, so the family members became virtually free while still legally being slaves. We know that the Harris family, while free, likely had family members who remained in bondage.[8] When Joseph's father, Jacob Harris, died in 1847, he left behind considerable property of which his wife had use for life or until she remarried. In that case, the property was to be divided among their eight children.

The origins of Joseph's mother, Charlotte Dismukes Harris (1808-1913) are murky. Dismukes is not a common name, which suggests she may have been connected to the family of Revolutionary War hero, George Dismukes of Chatham County, North Carolina. This was the only family of that surname in the state at the time of her birth, and their households are known to have included enslaved people. The 1850 census is the first one to differentiate between black and mixed-race individuals. Charlotte, then free and a widow, was listed as "mulatto." We know this because of the "M" after her name in the Census.[9] After her husband's death, Charlotte moved to Ohio with most, if not all, of her eight children.

"The family dynamics of business and social structure would change radically in the next generation. As the Harris siblings moved into white-collar occupations, their income may actually have decreased with the rise in status. We are told by family legend that Charlotte Harris moved her family to Ohio in order for the younger children to go to high school. Clearly there was a family tendency toward leaving artisanal labor for

---

[8] Ibid. Humphreys.
[9] Ibid.

the white-collar professions—teaching, preaching, doctoring, law."[10]

"In his account of free Blacks in North Carolina in the antebellum era, historian John Hope Franklin titled his last chapter "An Unwanted People." Franklin depicted a trajectory of the increasing oppression of free Black individuals, from the colonial period to the 1850s. In the early republic free Blacks could vote; some had earned their freedom by fighting in the American Revolution, although none were allowed to serve in the War of 1812. But as their numbers grew and fears of slave revolts escalated in the 1820s and 1830s, the relative tolerance of the free Black population gave way to paranoia and growing limitation of rights. The legal standing of free Black people became increasingly constricted. In 1826 the legislature decreed that justices of the peace could bind free Black children as apprentices if their parents were not taking sufficient responsibility for them. Initially apprentice masters were required to teach their charges to read and write, but the law was changed in 1838 so that it no longer applied to Blacks."[11]

While the Harris family was born free, the social construct in the Carolinas was a constant threat. A move to the north was desirable. After the death of his father (age 17), Harris moved with his mother Charlotte and family, by covered wagon over the Appalachian Mountains to the promised land of "free" Chillicothe, Ohio. J. D. worked as a blacksmith (consistent with a family of skilled tradespeople). In 1854 they moved on to Delaware, Ohio and to Cleveland in the 1860s.[12]

---

[10] Ibid. Humphreys.
[11] Ibid. Humphreys.
[12] Ibid. Humphreys. Page 45-46.

Joseph Dennis Harris, MD

The Harris family presents as Methodists; particularly African Methodist Episcopal (AME). The Methodist Church became a key component in the fight against slavery. Methodists leaders removed Bishops who refused to free their slaves. Methodists thought that Abraham Lincoln would usher in a great age of equality and freedom. Methodist ministers like the venerated Colonel Dr. Warner Renick Davis[13] left their pulpits and joined the Union Army in a fervor that could only be described like a Revival fire. "Mine eyes have seen the Glory!"[14]

However, there were Methodists who were not opposed to slavery. The differing views on slavery led to the creation of the AME in 1816 by Richard Allen. White Methodists established Wilberforce College in 1856 as the first institution of higher education in the United States specifically for African American students. The AME acquired the school in the 1860s.[15]

J. D. Harris knew French well enough to act as a translator while working in Haiti in the early 1860s. The English literacy of his family is itself intriguing; the fact that someone also taught him French is an even mightier mystery.[16] In Cleveland, Joseph began an unlikely rise to prominence as a physician. He also became intimately involved with the abolitionist movement, becoming an officer in the Ohio State Anti-Slavery Society.[17]

---

[13] https://www.findagrave.com/memorial/64264613/werter-renick-davis
[14] https://en.wikipedia.org/wiki/Battle_Hymn_of_the_Republic
[15] https://ohiohistory.libguides.com/religious/AfricanMethodistEpiscopal#:~:text=The%20African%20Methodist%20Episcopal%20Church,built%20in%20Ohio's%20major%20cities.
[16] Ibid. Humphreys.
[17] https://en.wikipedia.org/wiki/Ohio_Anti-Slavery_Society

Once J. D. Harris and his brothers left North Carolina, they joined the political antislavery and anti-discrimination institutions in the North. Such outspokenness would have been dangerous in North Carolina, but in Ohio some of them became what some might call downright "uppity" over time, engaging with the John Brown conspiracy and then escaping to the island of Santo Domingo to explore emigration possibilities for Black Americans. Cicero Richardson, sister Sarah's husband, was a known Underground Railroad conductor. Sarah was a printer in 1860 for an unknown newspaper. Perhaps it too was on the radical side. Two of her sons fought in the Civil War with the US Colored Troops. Rising through politics and revolution was a Harris family practice. J. D. would take that much further during and after the war. These family characteristics gave appeal to life in the North, but equally important was the "push" from southerners who wanted those free Blacks gone."[18]

In 1858 Harris joined antislavery activists, including John Mercer Langston, at the Convention of Colored Citizens of Ohio. Harris served as secretary of the convention and was named to the executive board of the newly organized Ohio State Anti-Slavery Society, for which he served as a lecturer in 1859 and vice president in 1860. The meeting was held in November in Cincinnati, Ohio. As an officer of the Anti-Slavery Society, Harris traveled to the Caribbean in search of sites suitable for settlement by African Americans who wished to leave the country.[19] Harris dreamed of a "Afro-American empire, where educated Blacks could lead the Caribbean islands to Protestant sobriety, modern farming, and settlement of African peoples. He argued that modern farming techniques

---

[18] Ibid. Humphreys.
[19] Virginia Humanities Encyclopedia. J. D. Harris (1833-1884).

would provide great advantages for relocated Black Americans. He worked to establish a colony for Black emigrants in the Artibonite Valley of Haiti."[20]

Harris wrote a book about his experience titled *A Summer on the Borders of the Caribbean Sea*.[21] The book described his trip to Haiti and nearby islands and advocated the establishment of a settlement for free blacks with the support and protection of the American government. The book received a long and favorable notice in the New York Evening Post on October 9, 1860.[22]

Harris was described in a friendly article in a Cleveland newspaper in 1860 as "quite an intelligent and enterprising slightly colored gentleman" and in an unfriendly article in a Richmond newspaper in 1869 as "a bright mulatto" whose "intelligence cannot be denied." By November 1860 he became an agent for the Haitian Bureau of Emigration for the State of Ohio. He traveled around Ohio and Canada advocating emigration before settling in Haiti in 1861.

In 1862, Harris returned from Haiti after the failed effort to establish a colony for free black people. He found a nation engaged in Civil War. The American Civil War environment lessened the prohibitions against black medical students opening opportunity for Harris to study medicine. In 1863 Harris matriculated at Western Reserve College (now Case Western Reserve University)[23] which was in walking distance to his

---

[20] Ibid. Humphreys. Page 8.
[21] https://www.gutenberg.org/ebooks/53418
[22] Virginia Humanities Encyclopedia. J. D. Harris (1833-1884).
[23] https://en.wikipedia.org/wiki/Case_Western_Reserve_University

mother's home. Records show that Harris had letters of reference from his professors John Long (the school's first dean), Dr. Jared Kirtland and Dr. Henry K. Cushing.[24] Then he progressed to the College of Physicians and Surgeons in Keokuk, Iowa,[25] completing his medical training in 1864.[26] In June of 1864, Harris became acting assistant surgeon assigned to the U.S. Army's Balfour Hospital in Portsmouth.

For the last year of the American Civil War, he served as a Union Army Assistant surgeon. His work for the U.S. Army settled him in Virginia.[27] During his tenure there his responsibilities increased from managing one ward with 100 patients to managing three wards. After the American Civil War Harris moved to the army's Howard Grove Hospital, near Richmond which treated African American soldiers and freed people. More than 10,000 surgeons served in the Union Army. Only 14 are known to be Black.[28]

Am I Not a Man and a Brother[29]

As the Civil War neared its end, Congress established the Bureau of Refugees, Freedmen, and Abandoned Lands — better known as the Freedmen's Bureau — inside the War Department. On October 1, 1865, Harris joined the Bureau of Refugees, Freedmen and Abandoned Lands.[30]

---

[24] Ibid. Humphreys. Page 138.
[25] Virginia Humanities Encyclopedia. J. D. Harris (1833-1884).
[26] https://www.lostcolleges.com/keokuk-medical-college
[27] Virginia Humanities Encyclopedia. J. D. Harris. 1833-1884.
[28] Ibid. Humphreys. Page 4.
[29] https://shec.ashp.cuny.edu/items/show/579#:~:text=This%20medallion%20was%20created%20by,symbol%20of%20the%20abolitionist%20movement.
[30] Ibid.

The Bureau was led by **General Oliver O. Howard** known as the ***Christian General***.[31]

"The Freedmen's Bureau helped tens of thousands of formerly enslaved people and impoverished whites in the Southern States and the District of Columbia in the years following the war. It helped freed people establish schools, purchase land, locate family members, and legalize marriages. The Bureau also supplied necessities such as food and clothing, operated hospitals, and temporary camps, and witnessed labor contracts between freedmen and plantation owners or other employers. Funding limitations and deeply held racist attitudes forced the Bureau to close in 1872. African Americans were abandoned to contend on their own with persistent racial attitudes and discrimination. Many continued to work for their former masters as sharecroppers or tenant farmers in a vicious cycle of debt peonage."[32]

Harris' move to Virginia during Reconstruction propelled his life to significance. His brothers William and Robert were prominent in the social construct and in the AME church.

Howard's Grove Hospital

These alongside the ladies sent by the largest Anti-slavery organization in the North; the American Missionary Association (AMA) worked as teachers and preachers to freed people. In 1864, Harris served as a U.S. Surgeon at Portsmouth, Virginia. Here the Union Army had converted a hotel into a "colored" hospital for USCT men and freedmen from the area.

---

[31] David Thomson, "Oliver Otis Howard: Reassessing the Legacy of the 'Christian General'," *American Nineteenth Century History* 10 (September 2009), 273–98.

[32] https://www.archives.gov/education/lessons/freedmen#:~:text=The%20Freedmen's%20Bureau%20provided%20assistance,family%20members%2C%20and%20legalize%20marriages.

These Virginians were stunned, and one is quoted as saying, *"There's a n____ doctor in Portsmouth in the capacity of a U.S. Surgeon."* Harris skillset presented his ability as a "second to no surgeon".[33]

Dr. Joseph Harris, a free-born physician, began working at the Fredericksburg hospital known as Howard's Grove Hospital for the Freedman's Bureau in December 1865 and remained there until November 1867. Howard's Grove Hospital had its own laundry, bakery, storehouses, water supply, and recreational facilities. It had a total of 62 buildings.[34] Next, he became assistant surgeon at the Freedmen's Bureau hospital at Fort Monroe in Hampton.[35]

Harris for Lieutenant Governor of Virginia

"Harris became active in politics, beginning with his signature on the call for a national convention of African Americans published in the Boston *Liberator* of September 16, 1864. The meeting was held three weeks later, although he did not attend. Harris probably attended some of the local and state conventions that African American men in Virginia held in the years immediately following the Civil War, and he attended and briefly spoke at a Richmond conference of black and white Republicans in August 1867."[36]

He ran as a candidate for the Republican Party's *radical* faction in the election of 1869. Harris entered public life late in the 1850s, advocation African American repatriation to the Caribbean.[37] Politically active and known for his intelligence,

---

[33] Christian Recorder. July 2 1864.
[34] https://www.civilwarrichmond.com/hospitals/howard-s-grove-hospital
[35] Virginia Humanities Encyclopedia. J. D. Harris. 1833-1884.
[36] Ibid.
[37] Virginia Humanities Encyclopedia. J. D. Harris. 1833-1884.

he received the Republican's nomination for lieutenant governor in the first statewide election under the Constitution of 1869. His multiracial background played a role in splitting the party that year. Nominated for the office of Lieutenant Governor of Virginia on the ballot with Military Governor, Henry Horatio Wells 1868/69.

"Harris's race instantly became one of the most-discussed aspects of the campaign. He acknowledged in an address to a state convention of African Americans on May 28 that some white Republicans would refuse to support the ticket as long as he was on it. Harris also advised black men to rely on themselves and not trust white men who had not clearly demonstrated their devotion to the interests of African Americans. Opposition newspapers condemned Harris because he had married a white woman, with the implication that if the radical ticket prevailed, interracial marriage would be part of Virginia's future. Those opposed to the ticket also raised the possible scenario that if the radicals won the election, the General Assembly could elect Wells to the U.S. Senate, leaving Harris to succeed him automatically as governor."[38] A breakaway group known as the True Republicans received the tacit support of the Conservative Party and carried the election.[39] Harris lost by 18,000 votes.[40]

"Dr. Harris strove to be recognized as a gentleman. Harris wore suits, was educated, and could speak well. When he ran for Lieutenant Governor of Virginia in 1869, he was turned away from white hotels and had to lodge at the 'Negro"

---

[38] Ibid.
[39] Virginia Humanities Encyclopedia. J. D. Harris. 1833-1884.
[4040] https://www.wikitree.com/wiki/Harris-39872

boardinghouse while his running mate acting governor never invited him to his home at the Governor's mansion."[41]

In his later years, he continued to work on bringing social justice. He practiced medicine in South Carolina, Virginia, and Washington, DC, before suffering a mental breakdown in 1876.[42] Sinking into mental illness, he was admitted to the Government Hospital for the Insane (later Saint Elizabeth's Hospital) in 1877. He died in 1884 in Washington, DC.[43] His then 13-year-old daughter and 10-year-old son, likely had only faint memories of their heroic father.

Maternal Heritage

Elizabeth Worthington was born on March 30,1840. in Milford, Michigan. Her parents were the Reverend Albert Worthington, (a Presbyterian minister), and Ruth (Parker) Worthington. Worthington's are a well-established family that included, Thomas Worthington, the 6th Governor of Ohio[44] (a man very active in the abolition movement) and Elizabeth's Uncle, George Worthington who built a hardware empire in Cleveland, Ohio. The paternal line has been traced back to 1642 in America and the 11th Century Lancaster England. The Reverend Albert Worthington was a graduate of Princeton Theological Seminary class of 1830.[45]

History has well documented the family's commitment to ending slavery with Thomas Worthington not only emancipating his slaves but also provided assistance and opportunity for them after their emancipation. After serving as

---

[41] Ibid. Humphreys. Page 15-17.
[42] https://www.lva.virginia.gov/public/dvb/sources.asp?b=Harris_Joseph_Dennis_1833-1884
[43] Virginia Humanities Encyclopedia. J. D. Harris. 1833-1884.
[44] https://en.wikipedia.org/wiki/Thomas_Worthington_(governor)
[45] Ibid. Humphreys. Page 164.

Governor, Thomas Worthington was elected Senator and took some of his emancipated slaves with him to Washington, DC as paid staff.[46] Worthington, Ohio is named in his honor.[47]

Elizabeth was a born in Michigan, while her Presbyterian minister father served a term of mission service. Throughout her childhood, he pastored in Pennsylvania and New Jersey. Both of Elizabeth's parents hailed from New England families.

Alumnae Hall was the second building to be built on The Western Female Seminary's campus in 1892.

Elizabeth was educated at Western Female Seminary in Oxford, Ohio founded by teachers from Mount Holyoake College in Massachusetts. She received her teacher training at Cortland Academy in Homer, NY. As a reference, Herman H. Sanford (one of her teachers) wrote, *"Miss Lizzie P. Worthington having been under my instruction, I most heartily recommend her as a faithful student, an earnest Christian and as one who in my estimation is eminently qualified & adapted to the work of a teacher."*[48]

Teacher, Singer, Musician

Elizabeth's father wrote her a reference letter for her application to the American Missionary Association (AMA). *"This certifies that my daughter Elizabeth is well qualified for the department of a teacher, both religiously and intellectually. She has enjoyed a thorough course of training in some of the best literary Institutions in our country. As a Christian, she is very*

---

[46] History of Ohio. Volume 2. Page 32.
[47] https://en.wikipedia.org/wiki/Worthington,_Ohio
[48] Herman H. Sanford, Corland Academy, Homer. Letter of Recommendation for Elizabeth Worthington, June 10, 1864. AMA Archives. Ibid. Humphreys. Page 165.

much devoted to the interests of her dear Redeemer's cause, taking an active part in Sabbath schools and Bible Classes. I can confidently recommend her not only in these respects as a teacher, but also as proficient in music. She is an excellent singer and can play well on any instrument. She is a member in good standing of the Presbyterian church.[49]

In the fall of 1864, she set out for her new post in Portsmouth, Virginia, escorted by one Robert Harris (younger brother to Dr. J. D. Harris). She earned $10 a month plus traveling expenses. The record shows that this devout woman tithed from her income to the AMA. She presents as a headstrong woman, raised in an prosperous family.[50] Elizabeth taught on staff with Reverend William D. Harris (brother to Dr. J. D. Harris) in the spring of 1865. At the same time J. D. Harris was employed at the hospital there in Portsmouth as a contract surgeon for the Portsmouth Hospital and his brother was the preacher.[51] As a single woman she was quite aware that more than 600,000 young men had died in the American Civil War.[52] This is of note as it greatly reduced the prospects for young women of marrying age.

In the Spring of 1865 Elizabeth wrote that she was quite pleased with the school and the progress of the children. She also asked to be transferred to a post in Richmond, Virginia. The request was denied. Elizabeth responded with a flurry of indignant letters. In these letters she expressed a litany of concerns and defense of her conduct, classroom activity and

---

[49] Albert Worthington regarding Elizabeth Worthington letter of recommendation. June 1864 AMA Archives. Ibid Humphreys. Page 271.
[50] E. Worthington to Whipple. June 10, 1864. E. Worthington to W. W. Whiting, February 9, 1865. E. Worthington to W. E. Whiting, March 31, April 29, 1865. AMA Archives. Ibid. Humphreys. Page 271.
[51] Ibid. Humphreys. Page 166.
[52] https://en.wikipedia.org/wiki/American_Civil_War

more. She apparently took exception to the supervisor, one Mr. Bell.

Despite her protests her next assignment presents as Morehead City, North Carolina in January 1867 under the Supervision of Mr. H.S. Beals. She taught 91 students with the help of her assistant, Mr. Jenkins. She wrote about the severe poverty of the children, their need for suitable clothing, no shoes or socks, and more. They needed chalk, blackboards, books, food and so forth. She asked for assistance with the rain, snow and wind that blew into the schoolroom and her lodgings. The abhorrent conditions of the post were no doubt heightened in her mind after the loss of her younger (and Harvard Educated) brother who died from tuberculosis that same spring.[53]

Elizabeth married Dr. Joseph D Harris on May 15th of 1868, in Goldsboro, Wayne County, North Carolina. The registry shows that the marriage was[54] performed by the Reverend William D. Harris, Joseph's brother and pastor of a large AME church in Richmond, VA. Somewhat oddly, the parents of the bride are listed, erroneously, as "James and Jane Worthington." North Carolina adopted Amendment 1 to their 1875 State Constitution prohibiting interracial marriages, but that was 7 years after this marriage took place. The bride, groom, and Rev William Harris were all living in Virginia at the time. The marriage took place in North Carolina as they had not, formally, passed anti-miscegenation laws.

The evidence available suggests that the marriage was a secret matter because of the legal barricades placed on Black Americans. The marriage of a white and Black was not a

---

[53] Ibid. Humphreys. Page 167-170
[54] https://encyclopedia.adventist.org/article?id=6JK6&highlight=y

casual event in Reconstruction society. "Miscegenation" was illegal in both North Carolina and Virginia. This was a blight that was not changed until the Supreme Court intervened in 1967.[55] No one in the Harris family seems to have lived in this location. In 2 letters in the AMA Archives written in June 1868 (a month after her wedding): she signed them "Miss Worthington" and they were mailed from her father's house in Vineland. The secret of the marriage was evidently being closely guarded.

In April 1869, the former Elizabeth Worthington finally signed herself, "Mrs. Dr. Harris." They were living in Hampton, Virginia in the third house on the right-hand side from the Hampton Bridge. There she wrote letters of reference for friends and co-workers, including Mr. Beals.

Elizabeth presents as being thrilled with her new title, "Mrs. Dr. Harris."[56] Her husband earned some 10 times what she earned as a teacher. She turned her attention to being a home maker. This was in line with her husband's rising status as a gentleman. After losing his bid to be Virginia's Lieutenant Governor, the Radical Republicans used their influence to have Harris appointed to a job as assistant Superintendent of the State lunatic asylum in Columbia South Carolina. He and his wife moved to nearby Charleston. The terms of his appointment were quite generous providing a salary of $1500 annually, plus a house and other expenses including funds to hire a servant.[57]

---

[55] https://en.wikipedia.org/wiki/Loving_v._Virginia#:~:text=Virginia%2C%20388%20U.S.%201%20(1967,Amendment%20to%20the%20U.S.%20Constitution.

[56] Mrs. Dr. Harris to E. P. Smith. July 13, 1869, AMA Archives. Ibid. Humphreys. Page 272.

[57] Humphreys. Page 199.

Elizabeth wrote a friend that her husband's new job as "The Doctor is Asst Physician-Head Attendant Treasurer & Secretary in our State Lunatic Asylum at a salary of $2000 & quite encouraging prospects for the future."[58] She may have exaggerated the number a bit to impress her friend or may have just included the other expenses in the totals. While Columbia, South Carolina was beautiful it had been quite devastated by the War. Elizabeth was in a fragile situation as a white, Yankee woman married (a marriage itself legally fragile) to a Black man living in a Southern state. Sadly, a new administration forced Dr. Harris out of his position by February 1, 1871. Harris publicly (published in the Columbia Daily Phoenix) expressed his indignation to the racially oriented dismissal.

Founding of Howard University 1867

Next, Dr. Harris accepted a position as a salaried obstetrics doctor in the Freedmen's hospital and the Harris family (now including baby girl Worthie) moved to Washington, DC. They bought a house on the corner of Seventh and Boundary Streets which also doubled as private medical practice. The area was a magnet for middle-class Blacks in general and African American physicians in particular. These formed the Black Medical Association (founded by Alexander Augusta, head of Howard's Medical School). Historian Margaret Humphreys noted that "Nowhere else in America was there such an aggregation of educated, professional Black men who would have shared many of J.D.'s ideas and perspectives." Howard University

---

[58] Mrs. Dr. Harris to E. P. Smith. March 28, 1870. AMA Archives.

became the center of Black medical care and education in the District.[59]

Following her husband's illness which led to his eventual institutionalization and death, Elizabeth remained in Washington, DC, where she raised her children. She lived on rent from her investments. She was the only surviving sibling of her generation. Her father gifted her with a modest amount of wealth after her marriage. Later, her father lived in their home till his death. Her husband helped her manage her investments including stock market, real property including several stores, the police station and life insurance.[60] Unfortunately, much of her wealth was mismanaged (which was blamed on Harris' illness) and some was lost in the Panic of 1873.

Langstone

John Mercer Langstone,[61] J.D.'s friend from Ohio and now Howard Law School Dean, told Mrs. Harris that J.D.'s mind was "shattered". There is no evidence that he was wrongly committed to the asylum. He died on Christmas Day in 1884 and was buried next to Elizabeth's father, Reverend Albert Worthington, at Graceland Cemetery, Washington, DC. He was fifty-one years old. In her will of 1898, Elizabeth stipulated that her husband and father should be moved to Woodlawn Cemetery[62] (Graceland was closing) and that she should be buried beside them.[63]

---

[59] Ibid. Humphreys. Page 203-204.
[60] Ibid. Humphreys. Page 206.
[61] https://encyclopediavirginia.org/entries/langston-john-mercer-1829-1897/
[62] https://woodlawndc.org/
[63] Ibid. Humphreys. Page 238-240.

In the late 1880s, Elizabeth was introduced to the Adventist message and in 1889 became a founding member of First Seventh-day Adventist church in Washington, DC.[64] A former Presbyterian, teacher in the Congregational Church of Christ oriented AMA and married to a Methodist strongly connected to the AME. The alliance with the SDA was part of a lifelong journey. Elizabeth died 19 Nov 1898, at the age of 58.[65]

The Washington DC Seventh-day Adventists were a formidable group. Seventh-day Adventism came to Washington, D.C., in 1886. Three years later, the first Adventist congregation in the city  was formed. Despite national racial conditions at the time, this church was integrated and socially progressive from the start. Rosetta Sprague, Frederick Douglas' daughter, was a notable active member. Around the turn of the century, however, during the Reconstruction era, this integrated Adventist congregation faced increasing pressure from both national politics and the General Conference to segregate. Thoro Harris' sister, Worthie Harris, followed her mother's example, joining the Seventh-day Adventist church around the same time. Whether Thoro was ever baptized into the Seventh-day Adventist church is unknown but likely. Elizabeth died in 1898..

---

[64] https://www.hmdb.org/m.asp?m=187421
[65] https://www.wikitree.com/wiki/Worthington-2198

Chapter 2

THE ARK IS COMING UP THE ROAD

Was such a thing really possible in the suburbs of Richmond, a Black doctor working in the heart of the Confederacy?… the hospital for freedmen…in the fall of 1865"…was neat, orderly and well located." Its managing surgeon was one, "Dr Harris, a very intelligent colored gentleman from Cleveland Ohio."[66]

---

[66] Ira Russell, "Report on Hospitals in Richmond, Norfolk, etc.," (1865), reel 3, frames 154-55, USSC Records.

Forging Their Own Way

Uniting their father's intellectual acumen and their mother's faith Worthie and Thoro Harris embarked on making their way in the post Reconstruction United States, Worthie seems to have led the way in the siblings' assimilation into white society. As children living with their widowed mother, they were identified as mixed race (1880 Census) likely prompted by their residential location in Washington, DC. Through her mother Elizabeth's extensive influence and connections, Worthie attended Dwight L. Moody's Northfield Seminary for Young Ladies.[67] It is evident that Elizabeth was focused both on education and ministry for her daughter.

From Northfield, Worthie transferred to Battle Creek College, in Battle Creek, Michigan, where she met her future husband, William Burroughs Holden, a physician like her father. After graduation in 1894, Worthie spent one year as a Bible worker in New York City. Holden's first poem printed in the *Advent Review and Sabbath Herald* was published while she was a student at Ballle Creek College in 1891.[68] It was a likely place for the young lady who was herself part of the founding of 1st Seventh-day Adventist Church in Washington, DC.

Worthie Harris married William Burroughs Holden on September 1, 1896. The couple had two daughters, Margaret Elizabeth (1898-1961), who married Dr. Edward Ellis Rippey, and Virge (March 28, 1906), who died at birth. Also, a graduate of Battle Creek College, William trained as a physician at the University of Michigan in Ann Arbor, Michigan, and Rush Medical College in Chicago, Illinois. While the couple lived in

---

[67] https://christianhistoryinstitute.org/magazine/article/the-northfield-schools
[68] Worthie Harris, "Our Consolation," *ARH*, January 20, 1891, 11.

Chicago, Dr. Holden taught at the Chicago Medical Missionary Training School.[69]

The newlyweds lived first in Battle Creek, then Chicago, where Dr. Holden taught at Dr. John Harvey Kellogg's[70] Chicago Medical Missionary Training School, and finally settled permanently in Portland, Oregon, where Dr. Holden was called to serve the Adventist sanitarium. Like Worthie's father, Holden was a surgeon.[71] He was a pioneer for what today is called Adventist Health.[72]

After enrolling in Northfield Seminary, Worthie never again identified as mixed race or black. Shortly before her death, 122 of her poems were published in a booklet entitled, *Songs for Our Pilgrimage*.[73] Worthie and her husband moved to Portland, Oregon, around 1903, where Dr. Holden taught at the Portland Sanitarium and Hospital, Worthie Holden served Central Portland Seventh-day Adventist church as deaconess and Sabbath School teacher, among other offices, until illness curbed her activity toward the end of her life.[74] Over the next thirty-three years, her poems appeared in the Review and other denominational publications such as the Canadian Union Messenger, the Pacific Union Gleaner, The Life Boat, and the Lake Union Herald, among others. Her writing focused on the Christian life,

---

[69] J. H. Kellogg, "The Chicago Medical Missionary Training School," *ARH*, December 10, 1901, 13.
[70] https://en.wikipedia.org/wiki/John_Harvey_Kellogg
[71] https://library.llu.edu/heritage-research-center/egw-estate-branch-office/seventh-day-adventist-biography-file?page=39&combine_op=contains&combine=&order=field_search_notes&sort=asc
[72] https://en.wikipedia.org/wiki/Adventist_Health_Portland
[73] https://www.waterstones.com/book/songs-for-our-pilgrimage/worthie-harris-holden/9781020653711
[74] https://encyclopedia.adventist.org/article?id=6JK6&highlight=y

encouraging trust in Jesus through life's trials and storms, and keeping one's eyes on the eternal goal of heaven. The last published poem appeared on the cover of the Review after Holden's death.[75] She died in Portland on March 29, 1921, of "chronic nephritis," indicating she may have suffered an autoimmune condition and kidney failure.[76] Worthie and her husband William, dedicated their whole lives the Gospel of Jesus Christ and the Seventh-day Adventist movement. They have their place in the history of the Seventh-day Adventists.[77]

Thoro Harris joined hands with the Seventh-day Adventist movement. Yet, his impact is much broader than one denomination. Several biographical sketches published in hymn histories state that Thoro attended Battle Creek College. Thoro was trained in music by his obviously talented mother who is recorded as being able to play nearly any instrument and was an accomplished vocalist. Thoro would use his talent and his training to teach music in Washington, DC at his alma mater Howard University. There he married a woman of mixed race, Agnes Hart (1876-1922) in March 1898. Their marriage license notice was printed in the "black" section of the *Washington Evening Star*.[78]

It presents that Worthie opened the door for her brother Thoro and his bride to join her and her husband in Battle Creek. He likely taught music in the nascent Battle Creek College. It is unlikely he moved there for educational purposes only and it is equally unlikely that the college would not have utilized

---

[75] Worthie Harris Holden, "Nearing Home," *ARH*, May 29, 1924, 1.
[76] Multnomah County, Certificate of Death no. 762 (1921), Worthie Harris Holden, Oregon State Board of Health, Portland, Oregon.
[77] Ibid.
[78] https://en.wikipedia.org/wiki/The_Washington_Star

both his teaching talent (and degree) and his otherworldly musical gifting.

While actively involved with the Seventh-day Adventist movement, Thoro produced his first Seventh-day Adventist themed hymnal in 1903 under the title *Echoes of Paradise: A Choice Collection of Christian Hymns Suitable for Sabbath Schools and All Other Departments of Religious Work*.[79] Charles H. Woodman of Boston was the publisher.[80] Thoro Harris compiled the volume. A copy is held by the Harvard College Library in the Harvard Divinity School Andover-Harvard Theological Library.[81] In the book, Harris acknowledges the "indebtedness due the Rev. J. E. Rankin, D.D.[82] for the free use of valuable copyrighted music."[83]

Chicago

Shortly after his first published work, Thoro and Agnes moved to Chicago, Illinois, at the invitation of Peter P. Bilhorn,[84] Bilhorn was a prolific hymn writer and evangelist who sometimes worked with **Billy Sunday**[85] and **Dwight L. Moody.**[86]He wrote some 2,000 Gospel songs in his lifetime. He invented the Bilhorn Telescope Organ, a folding pump organ used at revivals in the late 19th Century and founded the Bilhorn Folding Organ Company in Chicago.[87]

Billy Sunday & Peter Bilhorn

---

[79] https://hymnary.org/hymnal/EOP1903
[80] Ibid.
[81] https://babel.hathitrust.org/cgi/pt?id=hvd.32044017194580&seq=1
[82] **Rankin was President of Howard University.**
[83] Ibid.
[84] http://www.hymntime.com/tch/bio/b/i/l/h/bilhorn_pp.htm
[85] https://en.wikipedia.org/wiki/Billy_Sunday
[86] https://en.wikipedia.org/wiki/Dwight_L._Moody
[87] http://www.hymntime.com/tch/bio/b/i/l/h/bilhorn_pp.htm

In Chicago. Thoro compiled, edited, or produced at least fourteen hymnals, including *Light and Life Songs*, with William Olmstead & William Kirkpatrick (Chicago, Illinois: S. K. J. Chesbro, 1904)[88]; *Little Branches*, with George J. Meyer & Howard E. Smith (Chicago, Illinois: Meyer & Brother, 1906)[89]; *Best Temperance Songs* (Chicago, Illinois: The Glad Tidings Publishing Company, 1913); and *Hymns of Hope* (Chicago, Illinois: Thoro Harris, undated, circa 1922).

To the uninitiated this might just be a list of names and book titles. However, these men (William James Kirkpatrick, George Meyer, Howard Smith and others), were among the most prolific composers, organist, and musicians of their day. For example: Kirkpatrick became "a member of the Harmonia and Handel and Haydn Sacred Music Societies, where he heard the great singers of the day and became familiar with the principal choral works of the great composers. He is the composer of more than 50 Hymn collections.[90] Thoro Harris worked with the very best of the best. The connections that the Harris family made in the Chicago area forged the path for the rest of their lives.

Composer

Thoro was even more prolific as a composer. **More than 1000 melodies** are attributed to him, as well as the lyrics of over 800 hymns. Apparently, he worked on commission, as one hymnal, the *Blessed Hope Hymnal*, was published by the Advent Christian Church, and another, *Carols of Truth*, was

---

[88] https://en.wikipedia.org/wiki/William_J._Kirkpatrick
[89] http://www.hymntime.com/tch/bio/s/m/i/t/h/h/smith_he.htm
[90] http://www.hymntime.com/tch/bio/k/i/r/k/kirkpatrick_wj.htm

published by the **Pentecostal Herald**.[91] Regardless of who he worked for, Thoro's hymns focused on relationship with Jesus and the second coming.

Like his sister Worthie, Thoro and Agnes identified as white by the time they moved to Chicago, and all four of their children—Ulric (1902-unknown), Equador Saretta (1903-unknown), Jesse B. (1907-unknown), and Delna Preston (1912-before 1955) were described as white on their birth certificates. Although Thoro gained fame for his hymn writing, in the early years he did sometimes work as a carpenter to make ends meet. In 1930,

Retrospective

Thoro was obviously gifted a wide denominational exposure as a child. His uncles were fixtures in the AME church, his paternal grandfather was a respected Presbyterian pastor, both of his parents had worked for the AMA a Congregational Church of Christ oriented organization and his mother became a convert to the Seventh-day Adventist (SDA) movement.

Thoro's affiliation with the Seventh-day Adventist[92] denomination is nebulous. There is no report of his baptism, but during his teen and young adult years. He did maintain a relationship to the church as his mother was a founding member of the Wasthington, DC. First SDAHis first poem published in the *Review*[93] included this note, which suggests he believed in the seventh-day Sabbath while attending

---

[91] This Pentecostal Herald is the one published by H. C. Morrison who became President of Asbury Seminary.
https://place.asburyseminary.edu/ph/all_issues.html
[92] https://en.wikipedia.org/wiki/Seventh-day_Adventist_Church
[93] https://adventistreview.org/

Howard University: *"These lines were suggested because a fellow student had refused to read tracts bearing upon the Sabbath, alleging as a reason, that he might be convinced and have to obey"* (What I Might Have Known). His poetry regularly appeared in Seventh-day Adventist publications between 1896 and 1911.

After 1911 there is no evidence that he continued an affiliation with the Adventist Church. Rather, Thoro became closely aligned with Charles Parham's Apostolic Faith movement and evidence presents that they were personal friends.[94] He also worked with Apostolic Faith leader William Hamner Piper in Chicago.[95] Parham's meeting in (near to Chicago) Zion Illinois in 1906 was the catalyst for these connections.

Among the more than 1000 songs Thoro Harris composed is one he called *Coming up the Road* or *The Ark is Coming up the Road*. Thoro Harris presents as a child prodigy. Thoro was born while his father served in various roles as a leading doctor and surgeon in Washington, DC. Unlike what modern apologists would like us to expect, Thoro's family (although his father was of color and came from former slaves) presents as having been well to do. They "rubbed shoulders" with the upper echelon in Washington, DC. His father was a patriot, participated in the American Civil War and did his part to set a new path where all men were truly created equal. He was closely associated with many of the abolitionists of his day. The work they did was far from perfect, but it was a start. There will remain much work to be accomplished. Thoro's mother's family was white. However, neither his father nor his

---

[94] https://www.apostolicarchives.com/articles/article/8801925/173157.htm
[95] https://issuu.com/charismata/docs/apostolic_faith_and_pentecostal_tim_58f3c42b0a9f9b

mother was constrained in their spirit by the color construct that was prevalent in their day. Rather, they were reformers who practiced what they believed. A white woman, well placed in society, marrying a black man was rare, but that was the world into which Thoro Harris was born.

We have only a few glimpses into Thoro's brief childhood. We say brief because Thoro's father died when he was 10. At age 15 Thoro was already a student at the historic Howard University. The opportunity at Howard likely came about because Thoro's father had served as a physician for the Freedman's Bureau at Howard University and a plethora of the Howard Professors were personal friends. Thoro once recalled the cold wooden floors in their home as a child and having childhood measles. It was not a reference to an impoverished home. Quite to the contrary, his home was fine. All homes had cold floors on a winter night in the temperate Washington, DC area.

Thoro wrote his first melody at age 4 and by age 11 had his own system of musical notation. He played and took piano lessons at home. His mother, the formidable Elizabeth Worthington Harris was an accomplished musician; a gift she passed on to her children who were also gifted in music and composition (both poetry and hymns). In time, Worthie became an accomplished poet and Thoro became a phenomenal organist. He forged a path that musicians like Thomas Dorsey would later pattern.

Howard University[96]
Thoro's father died when he was a child of 10. The families' move to Washington, DC established connections in society that became beneficial to Thoro's widowed mother in the raising of her children. Not that it is of particular importance to this author,

---

[96] https://howard.edu/

but it is of general interest that in some documents Thoro is listed as a person of color and in others he is listed as white and still others as "mullata". Thoro attended the historic black Howard University (Washington, DC). He began his studies at the age of 15. At Howard University, Thoro recalled among other things taking formal music lessons, harmony counterpoint and musical form.

His commencement was in 1895. Howard President **J. E. Rankin, DD.,** presented him with his diploma. Jeremiah Eames Rankin (January 2, 1828 – November 28, 1904) was an abolitionist, champion of the movement, minister of Washington D.C.'s First Congregational Church, and correspondent with Frederick Douglass. In 1890 he was appointed sixth president of Howard University in Washington, D.C.[97] President Rankin was a friend of Thoro's father and encouraged the young Harris to continue at Howard University as a teacher in the music department. In 1896 Thoro was on staff at Howard University. On October 22, 1898, he married Agnes Hart from Charleston, West Virginia.

Agnes Harris

Battle Creek College

Battle Creek College

From Howard University Thoro and Agnes went to **Battle Creek College** to teach music in the growing Seventh-day Adventist movement in the area. Battle Creek was mecca to the Adventist movement. The principle of Battle Creek College was "race improvement through eugenics and euthenics." It was expected that all students, faculty, and staff would follow those principles—especially as regarding diet, exercise, and abstinence from smoking and drinking. School menus did not include

---

[97] https://en.wikipedia.org/wiki/Jeremiah_Rankin

meat. Kellogg's brother Will (W.K.) developed Kellogg's Corn Flakes and other cereals as dietary staples.[98]

Thoro Harris and his sister Worthie made eternal contributions to the lives of those connected to the SDA movement. His sister and brother-in-law were fixtures in the Seventh-day Adventist movement. Later, Thoro explained his exodus from the SDA and called what they offered "tyranny". Apparently, Thoro found his share of reasons to disagree with the practice of the Seventh-day Adventist ideas.

After becoming an adherent of the Apostolic Faith movement in the early 1900s, Thoro found his tribe'. In the Apostolic Faith movement Thoro did not have to hide his race or background. He was free in the Holy Ghost to live his life in Christ. In 1902, the accomplished composer wrote his first songbook. In 1903, the Harris family moved to Chicago, Illinois to work with a holiness minister and publisher. The Apostolic Faith movement and subsequent Pentecostal movement were the focus for the rest of Thoro's life. The move to Chicago was promulgated by Thoro's outstanding musical abilities as an organist and composer. The Chicago area was an epicenter for the Apostolic Faith Movement and the talented Thoro Harris was highly sought after. In Chicago, Thoro became involved in the Gospel publishing business. His connection to the Apostolic Faith movement would bring his songs to them and their songs to the world through publishing.

Harris next collaborated with the venerated **William Backus Olmstead** in 1904[99] and William Kirkpatrick to produce the first of two projects ***Life and Light***

---

[98] https://www.lostcolleges.com/battle-creek-college
[99] http://www.hymntime.com/tch/bio/o/l/m/s/olmstead_wb.htm

Songs.[100] *In 1914,* they did a second edition with the same title only adding No. 2.[101] Olmstead was a key leader in the **Free Methodist Church** at the time and had already produced the Free Methodist Church Hymnal in 1903. Later he and his wife became key leaders in the **China Inland Mission** with the Methodist Church.[102]

In 1907, Harris was the music editor for a book published for **Lemuel C. Hall** in Zion City, Illinois. Hall was a leader in Alexander Dowie's Christian Catholic Church in Zion. Hall moved to San Antonio, Texas to lead a church and soon became connected to the Apostolic Faith movement. About the same time, Thoro became associated with the prohibition movement and his songs were being used in Prohibition meetings. Prohibition would be a natural fit for his Holiness movement and Apostolic Faith connections as Charles Parham and others were often connected to the Prohibition effort.

Thoro's connection to Eureka Springs, Arkansas began with his close ties to the Apostolic Faith movement. Eureka Springs played an important role in the Apostolic Faith Movement. **Reverend Daniel Charles Owen (D.C.O.) Opperman** came to the Apostolic Faith in the early 1900s. He led a Bible College that was located in Eureka Springs and also published **The Blessed Truth**.[103] Later this town became the headquarters for a faction with an Apostolic Faith background that was called the General Association of Apostolic Assemblies (GAAA). The GAAA was an all-white group organized about 1917 and only lasted a couple of

---

[100] **Chicago, Illinois: S. K. J. Chesbro, 1904**
[101] **Chicago, Illinois: W. B. Rose, 1914**
[102] Ibid.
[103] https://www.apostolicarchives.com/Daniel_Charles_Owen_Opperman.html

years.[104] It does not present that Thoro was a direct part of this faction, but they certainly used his music and song books.

The 1910 United States Census has the Thoro Harris family living in Chicago with their three children (sons Ulrich and Jesse & daughter Ecuador Saretta "Margaret" Harris). Ecuador later changed her name to Margaret wondering what her parents were thinking when they named her.

Thoro Harris at his piano

Over the next decade Harris published a plethora of songs and song books. In 1916, Thoro hosted the founder of the Apostolic Faith movement and father of the modern Pentecostal Movement, **Charles Fox Parham,** at a meeting in Chicago, Illinois.[105] Thoro Harris was not just a song writer and publisher. He is often billed as an evangelist in the meetings in which he participated.

In 1922, Thoro's wife and mother of his 4 children Agnes died from smallpox. In 1923, Thoro married the second time to Isabel Godell from Nebraska. Little is known about this marriage. They divorced in 1925. In 1927 Thoro married the third time to Freda Walters. She was a woman from German descent who came to the United States to live with an aunt. Some speculate they met when she first became Thoro's housekeeper.

---

[104] https://www.apostolicarchives.com/articles/article/8795236/172426.htm
[105] https://www.amazon.com/Legacy-Charles-Sarah-Eleanor-Parham/dp/195225325X/ref=sr_1_11?dib=eyJ2IjoiMSJ9.no4JqTPwYQ6mNir1iC1X3x3di7ttsGaMpnP-O98tiQzyjhCeHHVojrn4gCREpp7OsYAkUZCMjRK8j478R-MwIS20kYjjaKxsodpUuyLmsBuBV0tGIH7iNogT-q7kIDJ_jRa77F59UYdFZOD019UiJzYORMuG4vy0qFhr2CJw5pasVuaJpeQDmnHxhMibpooC.xjB_AVKb-SBzjDUaCXovojlyPEu7cwnALfO6IRASyjM&dib_tag=se&qid=1734290588&refinements=p_27%3ABernie+L+Wade&s=books&sr=1-11

She is buried near him in Eureka Springs, Arkansas. Freda passed December 28, 1936.[106] In 1925 Thoro published the hardcover volume, the **Gospel in Song** for the **National Bible Institution** in Oregon, Illinois. In 1928 he published **Songs of His Coming**.

Apostolic Faith Headquarters Baxter Springs, KS

In 1930, Thoro led a meeting as an evangelist and is assisted by Rev. L. W. Triplett (billed as the Babe Ruth of the Gospel) in Revival services in Rock Island, Illinois.[107] Triplett is a regionally known minister who capitalized on the fame of the baseball player Babe Ruth. In Eureka Spring Thoro published another Hymnal: *New Songs of Praise*. The book is a mixture of his own music and that of other authors and composers. He also publishes a book called *Revival Gems* for KVOO radio (Broadcasting for Jesus).

In 1934, proving his long bona fides as a leader in the Apostolic Faith movement, Thoro Harris headlined what was believed to be the **largest Apostolic Faith meeting** ever.[108] Thoro had long been faithful to his friendship with the Parham family and the Apostolic Faith movement. The historic meeting was held in Baxter Springs, Kansas.[109] **Robert Lee Parham** (son of Charles F. & Sarah Parham) and his wife Paula were the leaders of this effort.[110] In 1936 he was a guest lecturer on music composition at Central Bible Institute, Springfield, Mo.

---

[106] https://www.findagrave.com/memorial/98135563/freda_harris
[107] Rock Island Argus. June 30, 1930.
[108] https://issuu.com/charismata/docs/apostolic_faith_and_pentecostal_tim
[109] Miami (Oklahoma) News Herald. August 5, 1934.
[110] https://www.findagrave.com/memorial/20595341/robert-lee-parham

In 1937 Thoro married **Rubye Bryant**. Rubye was his personal secretary as well as a song writer in her own right. Rubye was the daughter of Robert Crocker and Mary E. Bryant.[111] In 1941 Thoro published a new Praise and Worship Hymnal. Harris apparently did quite well financially and is remembered as being very benevolent toward other people and was once frauded out of all his money, but he persevered.

Rubye Bryant Harris

In 1943 he published *Songs of the Summerland* through his company, **Hope Publishing Company**. He was also appointed to the Board of Governors of the Church of Spiritualist the same year.[112] Thoro and Rubye lived in and managed the spacious **Piedmont House**. They ran it as a boarding house. Today, the house is used as a Bed & Breakfast. Residents of Eureka Springs remembered him. Many did not know or realize that he was a man of color. He played the organ at the Methodist and Christian Church in Eureka Springs. From all accounts he is one of the highly regarded citizens of the town.

Thoro Harris at Central Bible Institute 1936

Thoro Harris was a member of the ***Ozark Writers and Artists Association*** which is a *Who's Who* of talented people in the region. In 1945 he was billed thus: *"Thoro Harris has written more songs and edited more books of songs than any man now living."*

Noted Song Publisher Visits Alton
Thoro Harris, musical composer and publisher of onsiderable eminence, spent today at the home of Rev. A. W. Kortkamp on Hillcrest and it is probable that he will return to Alton tomorrow to sing some of his famous compositions at the Gospel tabernacle tomorrow evening. Mr. Harris is a prolific song writer and is head of the publishing house at Chicago that bears his name. He was en route today to St. Louis on a business matter and he was not certain that he would be able to come to Alton tomorrow.

---

[111] https://www.findagrave.com/memorial/49922649/rubye_harris
[112] November 8, 1943.

Chapter 3

APOSTOLIC FAITH LEADER

Charles Fox Parham

While Thoro Harris is associated with a plethora of movements, church denomination and organizations, he was aligned with the Apostolic Faith Movement for some 50 years. In the early 1900s Harris became connected with the Apostolic Faith Movement when Charles Fox Parham brought his Revival Tent to Zion Illinois[113] for a powerful outpouring led by Lilian Thistlethwaite.[114] Thoro remained connected to the Apostolic Faith movement for the rest of his life. Harris is closely connected with several prominent Apostolic Faith ministers and ministers with Apostolic Faith background. No doubt his ability to compose and publish was highly sought after.

After the Apostolic Faith movement was fractured by the defection of white supremacist ministers to form the Assemblies of God (AG), Thoro Harris continued his alignment with Charles Parham's Apostolic Faith movement. As his father was a man of color; Thoro was annoyed by the racial over tone of AG. By the time of the formation of the all-white AG, Harris had already endured decades of racial abuse.

Racial inclusion was the reason for his initial attraction to the Seventh-day Adventist movement. His mother's family and his father were forefront in the fight for ending racism and the hope of providing equality for all people; especially descendants of former slaves. Thoro was not faint to stand for right.

Around 1907 the division began in the Apostolic Faith movement. Howard Goss and his friends made many claims

---

[113] https://www.apostolicarchives.com/articles/article/8801925/173173.htm
[114] https://www.bu.edu/missiology/missionary-biography/n-o-p-q/parham-charles-fox-1873-1929/

and began an elaborate campaign about the reasons for their championing the idea of a new Apostolic Faith group only for white people. Much to the distain of white supremacists like Goss and his close friend W. F. Carrothers; Charles and Sarah Parham, who founded and led the Apostolic Faith Movement, continued to embrace people of all color as equals. This was not acceptable to those who did not see blacks as their equals. Southern whites and their sympathizers expected blacks, Mexicans, women and others to "continue in their place".[115]

The Parham's insistence of seeing black, Mexicans and others as equals was more than these were willing to bear. Howard Goss moved his new concept into a white supremacist position claiming to be the white faction of Church of God in Christ. Without evidence many historians call this the "White COGIG". More than 100 years later the evidence of Goss' claim is so scant it presents like gravy made from the shadow of a starving chicken.

Harris continued to be openly supported by the Parhams and the Apostolic Faith Movement, but also continued to sell his music and books to the other faction. In 1914 Thoro Harris edited and published a new song book, **Songs of Power**. L. C. Hall & J. O. Olsen contributed to the volume. L. C. Hall and E. N. Bell promoted the sales of the book. Hall was a pastor in San Antonio and Bell was an influencer who published *Word and Witness*.[116] All of the men had commonality in the Apostolic Faith Movement. Hall was a client of Harris' Glad Tiding Publishing Company in Chicago. Bell and Harris met in

---

[115] https://www.merriam-webster.com/dictionary/keep%20%28someone%29%20in%20his%2Fher%20place#:~:text=idiom,keep%20women%20in%20their%20place.
[116] https://www.apostolicarchives.com/articles/article/8795590/172502.htm

Chicago at the historic Stone Church.[117] Bell was destined to lead the Assemblies of God.

Stone Church in Chicago was key in the Apostolic Faith movement from the late 1906 to around 1940 when they joined the Assemblies of God. On December 29, 1911 the founder William Hamner Piper died from infection.

Rev. David Wesley Myland

David Wesley Myland (1858-1943)[118] was one of the founders of the Christian Missionary Alliance (CMA) denomination. He left the group over the controversy of speaking in other tongues. Like many of his former associates in the CMA, he became associated with the Apostolic Faith movement. He was the featured speaker multiple times in the years 1908 to 1912. He was the keynote speaker at an Apostolic Faith convention held at the Stone Church in Chicago in May through June of 1909. At this convention, Myland presented a series of lectures on the 'Latter Rain' and the Pentecostal outpouring.

Nellie & David Myland circa 1930

"This series of homiletical lectures, which was a sweeping and lengthy exposition of the Old and New Testament, was first published in The Latter Rain Evangel, which was edited by William Hammer Piper, the pastor of the influential Stone Church. These lectures were then published in book form in 1910 with the title 'The Latter Rain Covenant and Pentecostal Power: With Testimony of Healings and Baptism.' This book became the classical definitive apologetic for the validation of the Pentecostal outpouring as the fulfilment of the expected 'Latter Rain'. Alexander A. Boddy of Sunderland, England

---

[117] https://thestonechurch.org/who-we-are/
[118] https://healingandrevival.com/BioDWMyland.htm

wrote that Myland's book should 'be found in every Pentecostal home because it is an invaluable work of reference on the all-important subject of the Baptism in the Holy Spirit'."[119]

William Hamner Piper first opposed the Apostolic Faith, but after he separated from Zion in 1906, he invited Charles Fox Parham and other Apostolic Faith leaders to his church in Chicago. Stone Church became a mecca for the Apostolic Faith in the Chicago area. Here David Wesley Myland met Thoro Harris and together they complied a Hymnal in 1911. The Hymnal was titled **Gospel Praise**.

Under the thinly veiled guise of religion, racism is always at work. Piper's predecessor, William Durham, began a campaign that resulted in a formidable division in the Apostolic Faith movement. It is arguable whether it was by default or design, Durham devised a doctrine that pitted him against William Seymour. He eventually tried to forcibly take Seymour's church (the famed Apostolic Faith Gospel Mission on Azusa Street in Los Angeles, California) from him. This latter action prompted other Apostolic Faith leaders; notably Charles Parham and Florence Crawford[120] to defend Seymour. Parham went so far as to prophesy that either he or Durham would die. The die was cast. Whites and blacks were taking sides. Some months later the much younger and healthier William Durham suddenly died. Parham was a prophet. The white defectors hated him even more. They invested the next few years into

---

[119] https://revival-books.com/products/thelatterraincovenant-d-wesleymyland-ebook
[120] http://www.apostolicfaithmedford.org/

fine tuning their faction until they formed the all-white all male Assemblies of God in 1914.

Then in 1915, the group began a new fight. Some of Parham's followers insisted on baptizing like the New Testament Apostles by invoking the name of "Jesus Christ" in baptism rather than the titled version of "Father, Son, Holy Spirit" adopted by the Roman Church. In the end, there was even more division.

After the divisive events of 1910 and 1916 between the various Apostolic Faith factions, Thoro Harris made it clear his sympathies were with the Jesus name faction by introducing his new song, "Baptized in Jesus Name" at a 1916 Chicago meeting where Charles Fox Parham was the keynote. Many are unaware that in true Protestant fashion, it was Parham in the late 1890s who re-introduced the single name "Jesus Christ" baptism as opposed to the three titles of the Roman Church.[121]

It was the connection to Parham that brought such vivitrol against the Jesus name faction. Parham was opposed to all efforts to control the Apostolic Faith movement; particularly those who limited the role of women and people of color.

In response to those who opposed baptism invoking the name of Jesus Christ, Harris wore the opposition like a Red Badge of Courage and produced, **Songs of Jesus Only** from his publishing company 512 Campbell Avenue in Chicago. Yet, Thoro Harris, ever the entrepreneur, continued to sell music

---

[121121] https://cupandcross.com/wp-content/uploads/2016/02/voicecryinginthewilderness.pdf

and song books to the AG and others who may disagree with his theological conclusions and position. Music is a uniter.

April 9, 1916. Songwriter Thoro Harris is among the most notable participants at the **Lake Street Mission**. Chicago, Illinois. Charles Parham is ministering at Lake Street Mission. Thoro Harris, who is known as a black songwriter, said that when Parham preached the people loved the message and the messenger and looked forward to his (Parham's) return. Harris described the meetings as a "feast of good things."

Thoro Harris shocked the AG Council by being baptized in Jesus' name and would follow up with writing his song, "Baptized in Jesus' name." His baptismal hymn opens defiantly, "Today I gladly bear the bitter cross of scorn, reproach and shame; I count the worthless praise of men but loss, baptized in Jesus' name."[122]

Harris followed up in 1917 with his most well-known hymn, "All That Thrills My Soul is Jesus." The alliance between Parham and Harris at this meeting shows that Parham is still very much the leader of the Apostolic Faith movement. His working with Harris makes it obvious that he has some affinity with ministers that are baptizing in Jesus' name as opposed to the titles. Parham himself had baptized in Jesus' name stating that neither he nor his wife Sarah had ever been baptized using titles. In his book, **A Voice Crying In The Wilderness**, published in 1902, Parham deals with the subject of water baptism as it pertained to the doctrines of his Apostolic Faith Movement.

---

[122] Apostolic Faith and Pentecostal Timetable of Key Events. Volume 2. 1910-1920. Bernie L. Wade. 8th Printing 2024. Page 61.

Parham writes, "For years after entering the ministry, we taught no special baptism of water, believing the Baptism of the Holy Spirit to be the only essential one; having been marvelously anointed from time to time, and received the anointing that abideth, we put the question of water baptism aside. One day, while meditating alone in the woods, the Spirit said, 'Have you obeyed every command you believe to be in the Word'. I answered, yes; the question repeated, and the same answer was given. The third time the question was asked, I answered, no! for like a flood, the convincing evidence of the necessity of obedience rushed in upon me, how Peter said, 'Repent and be baptized every one of you in the name of Jesus Christ'. Was not this one baptism?"

"Then came the second; and ye shall receive the gift of the Holy Ghost. Again, Peter preceded at once to baptize Cornelius, and all his house, who had received the Baptism of the Holy Spirit, with the Bible evidence of speaking with other tongues. Thrusting aside all arguments, Peter replied, 'Can any man forbid water, that these should be baptized, which have received the Holy Ghost as well as we'. Paul did not recognize the baptism of John to repentance as sufficient, but rebaptized them in the name of the Lord Jesus Christ before he would lay hands upon them that they might receive the baptism of the Holy Spirit. These and other Scriptures were so convincing that the next day we were baptized by single immersion".

Parham continues by saying, "I can well remember when we sought God in this cleansing, how some of the teachings we had believed to be so Scriptural, and some we had loved so dearly were wiped from our minds. Among them was triune immersion; we could not afterward find a single argument in its favor. One day at the Bible School we were waiting upon God that we might know the Scriptural teaching on water baptism. Finally, the Spirit of God said: 'We are buried by baptism into His death'. Although we had known that for years, again the Spirit said: 'God the Father and the Holy Ghost never died." Then how quickly we recognized the fact that we could not be buried by baptism in the name of the Father, and in the name of the Holy Ghost, because it stood for nothing, as they never died or were resurrected. So, if you desire to witness a public confession of a clean conscience toward God, and man, faith in the divinity of Jesus Christ, you will be baptized by single immersion, signifying the death, burial, and resurrection: being baptized in the name of Jesus Christ".[123]

Garfield Thomas (G.T.) Haywood

Bishop G. T. Haywood was the renowned minister of Christ Temple Apostolic Faith Mission in Indianapolis Indiana. Originating as an Apostolic Faith Mission church, In time the ministry became known simply as Christ Temple.[124] While Haywood is credited as the founding pastor, he was actually the second pastor, but the most accomplished and the pastor who established the congregation. Haywood joins a long list of renowned ministers in the spiritual lineage of Charles Parham. After the AG leaders threated to lynch him and his friends in 1915, Haywood became to foremost proponent of the Jesus name movement. Some see his contribution as fuel to the fire for the white supremacist factions since Haywood was black.

---

[123] Apostolic Archives.
https://www.apostolicarchives.com/articles/article/8801925/173170.htm
[124] https://christtempleac.org/church/history/

Thoro Harris is the man that Bishop Garfield Thomas (G. T.) Haywood turned to for help in putting his songs to music and producing a hymnal. Most notable of these songs is Haywood's, "I **See a Crimson Stream of Blood**", but there are many others.

According to Pentecostal Historian, Dr. Gary W. Garrett, "My friend, Rev. Wes Arnold, explained that his pastor was **M. M. Hudson.** Hudson was baptized at the old Midway Tabernacle on February 2, 1928, in Mishawaka, Indiana. Bishop Glen Beecher (G. B.) Rowe was the pastor of this historic Apostolic Faith church. At a subsequent revival in Indianapolis (11th & Senate Street) on August 10, 1920, M. M. Hudson was seeking the Holy Ghost. When he did not receive the Holy Spirit, he felt that unforgiveness for some of his past discretions was the challenge. After consulting with Bishop G. T. Haywood, he sought resolution. However, the path he was advised to take for resolution did not bring relief for Brother M. M. Hudson. So, he went back to Bishop Haywood with more questions. In response, Bishop Haywood went into 7 days of fasting and prayer. At the end of that time, Bishop Haywood received the words to the song which speaks directly to dealing with condemnation and forgiveness."[125]

(L to R) Bishops Rowe, Smith, Haywood, Hancock & Rayl.

The year is 1920 and Bishop Haywood emerged from his study on a Sunday morning with this song in his spirit. Soon he traveled to Chicago to meet with the renowned Thoro Harris to enlist his help putting the song into music. According to Rev.

A D Urshan

---

[125] Credit. Dr. Gary W. Garrett. Apostolic Archives. www.apostolicarchives.com

Nathaniel Paul Urshan, after Haywood's meeting with Thoro Harris in Chicago, he went to meet with Pastor Andrew Urshan.[126] Haywood was excited to make him the first person with whom he shared his new song.[127] Andrew Urshan was a leader in the Apostolic Faith Movement. He later threw in his lot with those who adhered to the Jesus name baptismal formula causing his former 'friends' to distance themselves from him. Politics makes strange bedfellows. Religious politics has a capacity for creating enemies out of those who would be friends.

Fred Francis Bosworth

F. F. Bosworth was the Band Director at Dowie's church in Zion, Illinois. Bosworth was a self-taught musician who came from a devout Methodist family that fought to see their black brethren set free from the horrors of slavery. Bosworth began playing in a juvenile village band; then he played in the senior village band. When Bosworth was around 10 or 11 years old, his parents moved from Utica to University Place, Nebraska (a place noted for higher education among Methodists in the region). He became a member of the local band and then played a leading part in the Nebraska state band and local literary societies.[128] In Bosworth a young Thoro Harris found a friend and ally. There common love of music and God was the motivator. While Harris was subjected to dealing with racially motived would-be peers; in Bosworth he found a man free from the color construct offered by society.

---

[126] https://en.wikipedia.org/wiki/Andrew_David_Urshan
[127] Apostolic Faith Heritage Conference. Symposium. 2023. Joplin, Mo.
[128] https://en.wikipedia.org/wiki/F._F._Bosworth

Much has been written about F.F. Bosworth's relationship with prominent revivalists and Pentecostal church leaders. However, very little has been written about his work with African Americans. A famous photo shows a picture of him in a group with William J. Seymour. As it turns out, Seymour was one of only a few well-known blacks that Bosworth came to know. Another prominent and highly respected person of color that played a role in his ministry was **Thoro Harris**. Harris was a hymnist whose writing and publishing brought him name recognition and success. He and Bosworth shared a love for music. The two worked together during the 1920s.[129]

F. F. Bosworth

William Seymour

Bosworth used Harris' services to publish the songbook *Revival Flame: Bosworth Campaign Special*.[130] The extent of Bosworth's relationship with Harris is not known. However, given the quality of the book published, it appears that he fully endorsed the Ministry of Harris. The book consists of 138 pages. While 12 of the songs included were written or arranged by F.F. Bosworth, most were written by Harris. The significance of Bosworth's relationship with Harris is underscored by the fact that just over a decade earlier, Bosworth suffered a severe beating for preaching to blacks in Hearne, Texas. Also, during the 1920s, segregation was actively practiced in the United States.

---

[129] https://en.wikipedia.org/wiki/F._F._Bosworth
[130] **Revival Flame, Bosworth Campaign Special**. Publisher: Thoro Harris, Chicago, Ill., 1922. Language: English. Indexes. Authors · First Lines · Elements of Worship.

Through music Thoro Harris accomplished something that the rest of Christendom failed. While the Pentecostals were busy finding a plethora of reasons to divide themselves from one another, Thoro was selling his Song Books to all factions, groups and denominations. The Assemblies of God was not going to get left behind in the shuffle. They featured Thoro Harris Song Books in their Pentecostal Evangel like this one on 13 September 1924.

Harris, who has also been called a Pentecostal gospel songwriter and composer, was born on March 31, 1874, in Washington, D.C. His mother was white, and his father was black. Historian Dale H. Simmons described Harris as a child prodigy whose compositions in the Methodist Holiness style found appreciation among Pentecostals. According to Darrin J. Rodgers, director of Flower Pentecostal Heritage Center, Harris "was well-loved across the racial and theological divides within the Holiness and Pentecostal movements."[131]

Apostolic Faith Ministers John Adams, F. F. Bosworth, Thomas Hezmalhalch, William Seymour, John Graham Lake

In his article, *Remembering the Assemblies of God's Black Heritage*, Rodgers noted Harris' success in working with different church groups. He explained that Harris "moved seamlessly in both white and black circles, as well as in both Holiness and Pentecostal churches." Harris, he wrote, "made a substantial impact on Assemblies of God hymnody in its early decades."

---

[131] https://ifphc.org/About/Staff

Aimee Semple McPherson
Born Aimee Kennedy, she married Apostolic Faith preacher Robert Kennedy in August 1908. Aimee's parents were in the Salvation Army (but Aimee had shown little interest until she met Robert Semple). She heard Evangelist Robert Semple minister and after a brief courtship they married. They soon left for China as Apostolic Faith Missionaries. There Robert died leaving her with a child. Aimee used her Apostolic Faith connections to work William Hamner Piper with the Apostolic Faith Stone Church in Chicago working as an evangelist.[132] Charles & Sarah Parham had created rare opportunities for women to minister in the Apostolic Faith Movement and William Hamner Piper was like minded.[133]

Egalitarianism within the church has progressed slowly, quickly, or remained stagnant, depending on the denomination, but it has failed to reach the level of equality that secular society has achieved. "Women such as Florence Crawford and Aimee Semple McPherson came out of this movement and helped shape what the world knows as Pentecostalism today. Women's ministry involvement before the Pentecostal movement was very limited. Women could only serve in four avenues of church leadership: diaconate (nursing or social work), foreign missions, missionary societies, and Christian education."[134]

In 1915, Eudorus N. Bell ordained women based upon the Pentecost Proclamation, limited women to roles that would

---

[132] https://en.wikipedia.org/wiki/Aimee_Semple_McPherson
[133] https://christianhistoryinstitute.org/today/12/9
[134] Estrelda Y. Alexander, Limited Liberty: The Legacy of Four Pentecostal Women Pioneers (Cleveland, Ohio: The Pilgrim Press, 2008), 1.

not give them ecclesial authority over men.[135] Women could speak from the floor of the council, but they were not allowed to vote. Women could preach and evangelize, but only men could pastor and hold ecclesial offices of authority.[136] Women were only allowed to pastor churches if they had founded the church themselves. J. Roswell Flower agreed. In the all-white Assemblies of God, women lost the advancements that the Parham's had brought through the Apostolic Faith Movement.

Sister Aimee (as she was called) excelled and in many ways became the face of the Apostolic Faith movement. Or at least one of the faces. We must also consider the prominence of other women in the Apostolic Faith including but not limited to: **Lilian Thistlethwaite, Maria Woodworth-Etter, Florence Crawford.** Three things propelled Aimee Semple McPherson. 1. Internal strife of the Apostolic Faith Movement over racism and women's suffrage. 2. The insistence of Assemblies of God leaders like **J. R. Flowers** on using their organization for minimalizing the gifts and contribution of women ministers. 3. The death of William Durham which created a leadership gap in the ministries he led. Stone Church would align with the AG in 1916 but evangelist Amiee Semple McPherson moved in a different direction.

In was through her time in Chicago that she met Thoro Harris. In 1906 Harris had just compiled one of the historic volumes made for the organ. The book was titled Paramount Voluntaries for the Organ. It featured "works of Standard and

---

[135] Zachary M. Tackett, "Callings, Giftings, and Empowerment: Preaching Women and American Pentecostalism in Historical and Theological Perspective," in Women in Pentecostal and Charismatic Ministry: Informing a Dialogue on Gender, Church, and Ministry (Leiden, NETHERLANDS, THE: BRILL, 2016), 79, accessed October 14, 2020, http://ebookcentral.proquest.com/lib/seu/detail.action?docID=4731127.
[136] Ibid.

Classical Authors" and was arranged by the one and only Thoro Harris. The hardback book retailed for $1.50. The cover view showed an angel playing a harp. It was published by Meyer and Brother 106-108 Washington, Street, Chicago, IL.

Historian Estrelda Y. Alexander suggested Harris' work was respected by Aimee Simple McPherson, who often featured the singing of Negro spirituals in her church. In Alexander's book, *The Dictionary of Pan-African Pentecostalism*, she wrote about Harris' contribution to McPherson's ministry. She observed: "McPherson's regard for prolific African American hymn writer,[137] Thoro Harris, led her to work with him to compose at least two hymnals for the congregation." Among the volumes was the International Church of the Foursquare Gospel. Foursquare favorites compiled by McPherson, Aimee Semple, 1890-1944 and Harris, Thoro, 1874-1955. Declaration of faith contains 218 numbered hymns.[138]

1906

Raymond T. Richey

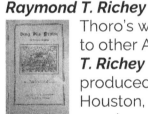
Thoro's work with Sister Aimee opened connections to other Apostolic Faith leaders including **Raymond T. Richey** and **Kathryn Kuhlman.** In 1936 Thoro Harris produced **Sing His Praise** for Raymond T. Richey in Houston, Texas published in Chicago. The same year he produced **Our New Song Book** published in Eureka Springs, AK.

---

[137] The Dictionary of Pan-African Pentecostalism. Estrelda Y. Alexander. *Volume One.* Cascade Books, 2018.
[138] https://oculyor.primo.exlibrisgroup.com/discovery/fulldisplay?vid=01OCUL_YOR:YOR_DEFAULT&docid=alma991005510329705164&lang=en&context=U

Chapter 4

HIS LIVING MUSICAL LEGACY

1. Abide in the Will of the Father in Heaven
2. All Glory to the Lamb of God
3. All My Journey Along
4. All Night the Slumbering Virgins Wait
5. All Our Days, Though Sad and Weary
6. All Praise to God That Man's Redeemer Came
7. All That Thrills My Soul
    a. Jesus är min högsta glädje
8. All the Way from Earth to Glory
9. Amid the Storm of Raging Fears
10. Among the Olive Trees
11. Answer Yes to Jesus
12. Are You Discouraged, Weighted Down with Sin?
13. Are You on the Gloomy Line?
14. Are You Pressing Onward in the Work You Love?
15. Are You Shining for Jesus, Your Savior?
16. Art Thou Weary, Broken Hearted?
17. As the Bow of Promise Gleams
18. As We Journey Along to the Homeland of Song
19. Ask for the Old Paths Saints of Yore Have Trod
20. At Times the Voice of Gladness
21. Attending the Rites of the Passover Feast
22. Awakening, The
23. Back in the Long Ago
24. Back to the Bible
25. Be Diligent and True in Everything You Do
26. Be Thou to Me, O Christ, a Sanctuary
27. Bearing a Load of Unforgiven Sin
28. Because from All Eternity the King of Glory Tho't of Me
29. Before the Sun Illumes the Day
30. Believe in the Word of Jehovah
31. Beyond the Silent Stars of Night
32. Blessed, Blessed Hope, Jesus Will Return
33. Blessed Gospel Wins Its Way, The
34. Blessed Invitation from the King of Heaven
35. Blessed Jesus Loved Me, The
36. Blessed Jesus, Tender
37. Blest and So Happy Am I
38. Blest Savior, Faith's Celestial Star
39. Bound for a Mansion in Beulah
40. Burdened by Sorrow, Whoe'er Thou Art
41. By His Kind and Gracious Favor
42. Can We Raise the Fallen from the Pit of Sin?
43. Can You Point a Soul to Jesus?
44. Caught Up
45. Cheer Up, O Fainting Christian, God's Blessing
46. Christ Is Calling Wanderers in the Far Away

47. Christian, Forget Not from Day to Day
48. Christian, Have You Proved a Slacker Today?
49. Citizen of Heaven, Dwelling Here on Earth
50. City All Fit Doth Jesus Prepare, A
51. Cling to the Life-line, Danger Is Near You
52. Come and Give Your Heart to Jesus
53. Come, Let Us Join Glad Hands and Cheerful Voices
54. Come Now from Your Slumber Awaking
55. Come, O Come to the Mercy Seat
56. Come, O Come with a Contrite Heart
57. Come On, Believer in the Lord
58. Come Sing with Me His Glory
59. Come Sinner, Come to Jesus
60. Come to the Fountain That Flows
61. Come to the Savior, O Sinner, Today
62. Come unto Jesus Thy Friend and Brother
63. Come unto Me, O Hear the Gracious Word
64. Come with Hearts and Voices Now and Sing
65. Coming Again
66. Coming for Me
67. Coming Up the Road
68. Could Any Spot on Earthly Sod
69. Craving Hope and Rest
70. Cuckoo Sings, The
71. Dark the Storm Is Raging
72. Day of Wrath, The
73. De Win' Blow Soft from de Heav'nly Sho'
74. Dead unto Sin but Alive to God
75. Deal with Me as Thou Wilt
76. Dear Son of God Once Left His Father's Throne, The
77. Don't Forget the Father Loves You
78. Dry the Tear and Weep No More
79. Earnestly, Tenderly Calling the Erring
80. Earth Has Many Scenes That Charm Me
81. Eternal Peace Will Soon Begin
82. Eternal Rest
83. Eternity, Eternity, How Near Art Thou
84. Evening Sun Is Setting in the West, The
85. Every Promise Is a Check upon the Bank
86. Exert Thy Power, O Glorious Savior
87. Facing a Future of Shame and Woe
88. Fairer Light Than Sun and Moon
89. Far from Jesus Long I Wandered
90. Father and the Son, The
91. Father, Hear Me While I Pray
92. Father of Mercy, Author of Salvation
93. Father, Remembers His Children Dear

94. Father, We Adore Thee
95. Finding Rest Amid Labor
96. For All God's Love to Man
97. Forth from the Heart of the Father There Came
98. Forward I Look to That Blissful Hour
99. Forward We Go, Facing the Foe
100. From Jesus I Have Wandered
101. From Sinai's Smoking Mountain
102. Full and Free Salvation the King Provides, A
103. Gently, Gently Kneel and Pray
104. Glory, Glory Be to God
105. Glory, Glory, Hallelujah
106. Glory in the Highest
107. Glory to God, Our Portion
108. Go Thou, My Chosen One
109. God Bless Our Home, and Fill It
110. God Hath Appointed a Ruler
111. God Is Calling Us to Move
112. God Is My Sure Protection
113. God Loved a World of Sinners
114. God of Grace Is Calling Thee, The
115. God Pities His Children
116. God Sent His Well Beloved One
117. God Who Formed Thee, The
118. God's Faithful Children Here Below
119. God's Holy Book Is Given
120. Gracious Master, Meek and Lowly
121. Great Wide World for Jesus, The
122. Groping Your Way Through the Darksome Night
123. Happy Are the Moments, Every One
124. Happy in Jesus, Trusting in His Grace
125. Hark, I Hear Ten Thousand Voices Sing
126. Hark, the Gospel Invitation
127. Hark, the Promise of the Savior
128. Hast Thou Some Friend Who Far Away
129. Have You Left the Fold?
130. Have You Met Sin's Mighty Host in Stern Array?
131. He Gives Me Joy, Joy
132. He Is Able to Deliver
133. He Leadeth Me, He Leadeth Me, with Him
134. He That Believeth Shall Nevermore Die
135. Hear the Gospel's Joyful Sound
136. Hear the Savior Pleading
137. Hear the Tender Story of Jesus' Love
138. Hear Thy Father Calling
139. Heralds of Day Dawn Go
140. He's Coming Soon

141. His Face Will Outshine Them All
142. Ho, All Ye Sick and Dying
143. Holy Is the Father, Holy Is the Son
144. Holy Lord, in Pure Devotion
145. Honor, Praise and Majesty
146. Hosanna to the Living Word
147. How Can the Heart So Prone to Stray
148. How Gentle and Sweet, Is the Savior's Voice
149. How I Long for Rest for My Weary Soul
150. How It Charmed Me and Filled Me with Gladness
151. How Sinless the Life
152. How Strangely Sweet Is the Story
153. How Wonderful Jesus Is!
154. How Wondrous Is His Grace and Condescension
155. How Wondrous Is the Crimson Tide
156. I Am a Child of the King of Kings
157. I Am Coming Home
158. I Am Dreaming Today
159. I Am Kneeling at Thy Feet
160. I Am Nearing the City
161. I Am Rejoicing Now
162. I Am Saved by the Blood Freely
163. I Am Thinking Today of a Friend Far Away
164. I Am Traveling on to Canaan
165. I Am with You, Spake the Master
166. I Came to Christ, the Savior
167. I Cannot Know All the Fullness
168. I Cannot Sing as Angels Sing
169. I Cannot Tell the Wonder
170. I Come to Thee, Savior
171. I Dreamed One Night I Was Standing Near
172. I Give Myself, My All to Thee
173. I Have a Kind Brother
174. I Have a Savior, a Dear, Loving Friend
175. I Have a Savior Who's Mighty
176. I Have Been All Alone with My Savior
177. I Have Caught a Revelation
178. I Have Entered
179. I Have Yielded All
180. I Hear Most Wonderful Melody
181. I Know a Chosen People
182. I Know a King Who Left His Throne
183. I Know Not What Waits Me Tomorrow
184. I Love Him Better Day by Day
185. I Love Him Better Every Day
186. I Love His Appearing
187. I Love My Gracious Savior

188. I Love the Name of Jesus Who Died
189. I Praise the Lord That a Savior Came
190. I Remember the Word Which So Often
191. I Rest in the Love of the Crucified
192. I Saw the Light
193. I Sing of Jesus, the King Immortal
194. I Sing of One Who Made Me Whole
195. I Trust in My Blessed Redeemer
196. I Wandered in Darkness
197. I Was a Hopeless Sinner
198. I Was a Lost and Wayward Child
199. I Was Drifting Far from Land
200. I Was Out on Life's Sea
201. I Will Look to the Hills
202. I Will Love Thee, O My Savior
203. I Would Not Choose My Pathway
204. If at Jesus' Call You Have Left Your All
205. If Jesus Should Summon the Nations
206. If One Should Ask Me Why
207. If Some Who Christ Profess
208. If Sorrows Fast Are Thronging
209. If You Have Started in This Race
210. If You Only Could Know Jesus Bore All
211. If You Would Be from Sin Set Free
212. If You Would Know Abiding Peace Within
213. I'll Be a Sunbeam
214. I'm a Child of God Forever
215. I'm a Little Pilgrim
216. I'm an Heir of the King
217. I'm Happy Every Sunday
218. I'm Praying for You
219. In All You Do Keep This in View
220. In Christ Let All the World Rejoice
221. In Country, Town or City
222. In Desert Wilds I Went Astray
223. In Earth's Wondrous Gallery of Pictures
224. In Glory Transcending
225. In Him Complete, O Praise the Lord
226. In Joseph's Tomb Mid Blackest Gloom
227. In My Distress to Him I Cried
228. In the Lands Beyond the Sea
229. In the Name of Christ We Gather One and All
230. In the Path of Sin No Longer Straying
231. In the Upper Room at Jerusalem
232. In the Yawning Pit of Sin
233. Into the Depth of God's Promise
234. Is Any Sick Among the Saints?

235. Is It Nothing to You That the Highest Came?
236. Is Your Life Aweary, Are You Tempted to Despair?
237. Is Your Life Fully Yielded to Jesus?
238. It Stands by Stream in the Wildwood
239. I've a Friend Above All Others
240. I've Enlisted for the King to Fight
241. I've Found the Way to Perfect Rest
242. I've Lived Far Down on Grumble Lane
243. I've Wandered Far o'er Sin's Dark Wild
244. Jehovah's Promise
245. Jesu, Name of Names the Sweetest
246. Jesus Bears You on His Heart
247. Jesus, Blessed Jesus
248. Jesus, Blessed One, God's Beloved Son
249. Jesus Christ, a Blessed Heavenly Stranger
250. Jesus Gently Pleads Today
251. Jesus, How Blest Thy Cross Appears
252. Jesus Invites You, Weary of Sin
253. Jesus Is Calling, Come unto Me
254. Jesus Is Calling for Soldiers Today
255. Jesus Is Calling the Wanderer Home
256. Jesus Is Calling the Wanderer Today
257. Jesus Is Calling You Back to Your Home
258. Jesus Is Coming, Our Long Watch Is Ending
259. Jesus Is Coming Soon
260. Jesus Is Coming, the Message Proclaim
261. Jesus Is Earnestly Calling the Lost
262. Jesus Is First of All to Me
263. Jesus Is My Heart's Eternal Treasure
264. Jesus Is True
265. Jesus, Jesus, Higher Than Highest Archangels
266. Jesus, Perfect Savior, Seated on Thy Throne
267. Jesus, Redeemer, Precious Though Unseen
268. Jesus Saves, Jesus Saves
269. Jesus! The Christ, God's Glorious Son
270. Jesus, Thou Living Bread, Broken for Me
271. Jesus, Thou Savior, Who Heard My Cry
272. Jesus Will Come to Earth Again
273. Jesus Will Return
274. John Saw the Multitude and Cried
275. Jonah the Prophet by God Was Sent
276. Joy Bells of Heaven Are Ringing
277. Just a Little Talk with Jesus
278. Just One Look at the Cross of Jesus
279. Just See That Sun, See How He Run
280. Keep Busy, Keep Busy
281. Keep in Touch with Jesus

282. Keep the Danger Signal Flying
283. Keep Under the Blood of Jesus
284. Keeping Back the Money of the King
285. King of Glory, The
286. King Will Stand Beside You, The
287. King's Highway, The
288. Knocking, Ever Knocking
289. Let Him In
290. Let Us All with Joyful Heart Proclaim
291. Lift Me Higher, Lord, All Gracious
292. Lift the King's Own Standard
293. Lift Up the Voice
294. Lift Up Thy Voice Like a Trumpet
295. Lift Your Eyes, Behold the Fields
296. Little Children, Praise the Lord
297. Little Man of Whom We Read, A
298. Living in the Spirit Every Passing Day
299. Lo a Penitent Voice
300. Lo It Is Finished, Resoundeth a Voice
301. Lo the Youthful Jacob on His Weary Way
302. Long This World with All Its Snares Depraved
303. Long We've Heard the Joyful Story
304. Look for the Beautiful
305. Look on Thy Little Ones
306. Looking for That Blessèd Hope
307. Lord Bade His Apostles, The
308. Lord, I Have Started to Walk in the Light
309. Lord Is Our King, Exulting We Cry, The
310. Lord Keep Watch, The
311. Lord, Let Me Be a Glass
312. Lord, Receive Me, I Am Coming Home
313. Lord to Earth from Heaven Came, The
314. Lost Was I in Sin and Degradation
315. Love That Jesus Bore to Me, The
316. Make the Earth Look Fairer
317. Many Are Turning to Jesus Today
318. Many Trials I Meet on My Homeward Way
319. Mercy Boundless and Free
320. Message of Mercy
321. Met in Their Master's Name
322. Mighty Gospel Wins Its Way, The
323. More Abundantly
324. Morning Breaks, 'Tis Bright and Clear, The
325. Multitudes Followed Our Savior
326. Multitude Thronged Him on Every Hand, The
327. My Father's House
328. My Heart Was Sad and Weary

329. My Life Is Filled with Sunshine
330. My Only Hope Is Jesus
331. My Savior Came Down from the World of Light
332. Nations of the World Have Pined, The
333. Nearer, Nearer, Every Moment
334. Never Failing Friend, The
335. No Heart Is Like the Heart of Jesus
336. No Matter How Strong the Chains That Bind Thee
337. No Separation, Now Made One
338. Nobler by Far Than the Sages of Earth
339. O Christian, in These Latter Days
340. O Come unto Jesus, and Trust in His Name
341. O Dear One for Whom Our Petitions Ascend
342. O Father Hear Our Humble Prayer
343. O Gracious Message by the Master Given
344. O Happy Land of Paradise
345. O Hear the Glad Message from Heaven Above
346. O Hear the Wondrous Story
347. O Hearken to the Gospel Warning
348. O Home of Fadeless Glory
349. O How Dear the Old Camp Meeting
350. O, I Am So Happy in Jesus
351. O I Know a Clime Genial All the Time
352. O Jesus, Lord, Remember Me
353. O List to the Message from Heaven Above
354. O Love from Whence My Mercies Flow
355. O My Soul Keeps Singing Hallelujah
356. O My Wandering Brother
357. O Praise Jehovah, Great I AM
358. O Soul in the Vale of Decision
359. O Speed with the Tidings from City to City
360. O the Cleansing Blood of Jesus
361. O the Land Beyond the Sea
362. O the One I Love Best of All Is Jesus
363. O the Sweetest Word Known to Mortal Tongue
364. O the Wondrous Consolation
365. O the Wondrous Power of the Savior's Love
366. O Weary Heart, There Is a Home
367. O Wounded Hearts, This Message Hear
368. Obey, 'Tis Better Than Sacrifice
369. Oil
370. Oil in My Lamp
371. On Him Who Watches Over All
372. On the Resurrection Morning
373. On Your Homeward Journey
374. Once I Heard the Story of Jesus' Love
375. Once I Saw in My Visions the Savior of Men

376. Once I Was Dreary and Not Content
377. Once I with Chains Was Bound
378. Once My Path Was Dreary
379. Once the Savior Trod on Our Earthly Sod
380. One Friend Divine Is So Dear to Me
381. One Hath God Ordained
382. One Knocks at Your Bolted Door
383. One Little Step to Jesus
384. One Standeth Outside at Your Heart's Bolted Door
385. One There Is Divinely Gracious
386. One There Is Who Longs to Save You
387. Onward Move, Ye Followers of the Lord
388. Onward We March to the Kingdom
389. Our Gracious Lord Came Down
390. Our Savior Soon Is Coming
391. Our Stay on Earth
392. Peal the Message Far and Wide
393. Peerless Name, The
394. Pentecost in My Soul
395. Perfect Deliverance
396. Pilgrim on the Upward Way, A
397. Praise Him, Praise Him
398. Pray on, Believer in the Lord
399. Prize, O Prize the Golden Moments
400. Promised Hour Is Drawing Near, The
401. Prophet of Old to This Countrymen Cried, The
402. Purpose of God Let Me Fulfill, The
403. Raise the Standard High
404. Rejoicing in Hope, Believing His Word
405. Remember, How, Before You Left Your Home
406. Remember Thou the Sabbath Day
407. Reveal Thyself, Great God of Power
408. Ring Out the Message of Glorious
409. Savior All My Foes O'ercame, The
410. Savior Is Calling the Wanderer Home, The
411. Savior Is Calling You into the Fold, The
412. Scatter Sunshine, Scatter Sunshine
413. See o'er Yonder Mountain Misty Clouds Arise
414. See the Spotless Lamb of God
415. Since First I Knew Redeeming Love
416. Sing, O Sing the Wondrous Love of the Christ
417. Sing of Truth, Welcome Truth
418. Sing the Blessed Story of the Prince of Glory
419. Sing We Songs of Joy and Gladness
420. Sinner, the Savior Is Calling
421. Soldiers, Tried and Faithful
422. Some Day Triumphant o'er the Tomb

423. Some Fair Morn I Shall Stand
424. Some Joyful Day
425. Some Work Is Surely Given
426. Somebody Sought Me When Far from the Fold
427. Someone Is Called by the Master
428. Someone Is Here with an Aching Heart
429. Someone Will Enter the Pearly Portals
430. Someone Will Go from This House of God
431. Someone Will Greet the Returning King
432. Sometimes I Grow Faint and Weary
433. Son of God Atonement Made, The
434. Son of God Hath Power to Recreate, The
435. Song of Love, A
436. Sons of Men, with Heart and Voice
437. Soon Jesus Will Come to Gather
438. Soon Our Lord from That Far Country
439. Soul, Are You Here with an Aching Heart?
440. Soul, Do You Hear a Kind, Loving Voice?
441. Standing Alone in the Judgment Hall
442. Still Saying No to Jesus
443. Stranger I to Fear, A
444. Stranger's Hand Is Knocking, A
445. Sun of Infinite Mercy Is Shining, The
446. Sweet 'Tis to Know in the Midst of the Storms
447. Sweetest Name in Highest Heaven
448. Sweetest Sound Mortal Ever Heard, The
449. Sweetly Sing, Sweetly Sing
450. Take Back Your Heart to the Savior
451. Take the Blessed Savior with You
452. Taken Aside by Jesus
453. Talk of His Power, Maker of All
454. Tell All to Jesus
455. Tell Me the Sweetest Story
456. Tell, O Tell the Blessed Story
457. Time Is Fast Approaching
458. There Are Lands Far Away o'er the Sea
459. There Are Many Snares and Dangers
460. There Is a Book, All Other Books Excelling
461. There Is a City
462. There Is a Dear Story I Love to Repeat
463. There Is a Fountain, a Sin Cleansing Flood
464. There Is a Place of Blessing
465. There Is a River Deep and Wide
466. There Is Hope for the World
467. There Is Need for a Mighty Revival
468. There Is One by Your Side Who Cares
469. There Is One Friend Believers Prize

470. There Is One Friend Ever Near Me
471. There Is Praise on My Lips
472. There Is Victory Through the Blood
473. There Was Never a Heart Like Jesus
474. There Will Be a Grand Convention
475. There's a Battle to Be Fought
476. There's a City Eternal Beyond the Deep Sea
477. There's a Crown to Win in the Fight with Sin
478. There's a Song upon My Lips
479. There's Glory in the Dawning
480. There's New Joy Within My Soul
481. There's No Earthly Tie Can Bind
482. There's Nothing So Sure
483. There's One Above Whom I Dearly Love
484. There's One Who Is Always Faithful
485. They Come
486. Think Not Your God Forgets You
487. This Great Wide World
488. This Sacred Truth Means More to Me
489. This World Is Far Too Dreary
490. Those Were Darksome Years
491. Thousands Are Trusting Jesus Today
492. Thy Savior Is Pleading, O Wanderer, Today
493. 'Tis God's Day of Pardoning Grace
494. 'Tis Joy to Work for Jesus
495. To Despair My Soul Was Almost Driven
496. To Every Tribe and Nation
497. To Jesus My All I Resign
498. To the Lord There Came
499. To Whom Can I Go?
500. Today I Gladly Bear the Bitter Cross
501. Too Long I Roamed
502. Too Long I Slighted Jesus
503. Trust the Eternal
504. 'Twas a Gladsome Hour
505. 'Twas Long Ago the Savior
506. Unto God Our King
507. Voice of the Spirit Is Speaking, The
508. Waiting on the Lord for the Gift from Heaven
509. Wanderer, Lost in Sin's Dark Valley
510. Wanderer on the Plains of Sorrow
511. Wanderer Out on a Desert Dreary
512. Washed in the Fountain
513. We Adore Thee, Holy Savior
514. We Are Bound for the Bright, the Shining Land
515. We Are Pilgrims on the Earth
516. We Are Watching for the Coming

517. We Build on the Rock
518. We Have Heard the Glorious News
519. We Know Not the Day and We Know the Hour
520. We Know Not the Day When the Master Shall Come
521. We Lift Our Cheerful Voices
522. We Would Cross Over the River
523. Wearied with the Vigils of a Fruitless War
524. Weary One, List to the Savior's Kind Voice
525. Weary One, Whoe'er Thou Art
526. Welcome, Day of Gladness
527. Welcome, Welcome, a Hearty Welcome
528. We'll Never Be Late
529. We're Coming, We're Coming, Dear Savior
530. We're Walking in the Light
531. We've Enlisted in the Fight
532. We've Heard of a City
533. We've Waited on Full Many a Year
534. What a Blessed Gospel of the Grace of God
535. What a Great and Wise Provision
536. What Did Isaiah Say Was the Rest
537. What Doth the Master Require at Thine Hand?
538. What He Has Done for Others
539. What Is the Church's Crying Need?
540. What Though the Storm Around Me Rage
541. What Treasure of Earth Can Equal in Worth
542. When Clouds Hang Dark Above You
543. When Earth with Her Trials Forgotten
544. When God's Own Hand Makes All Things New
545. When God's Sweet Spirit Made Me Know
546. When I Am Weary and Long Seems the Day
547. When I Had Weary Grown of Sin
548. When I Have Moved to Yon Heavenly
549. When Israel Out of Babel Came
550. When Jesus Came the Lost to Save
551. When Jesus on Dark Calvary
552. When My Poor Heart, Torn by Anguish and Pain
553. When Proud Amalek's Host Assailed
554. When Sad and Dismayed I Plead
555. When Samuel Wanted Money
556. When the Canaanites Hardened
557. When the Lord of Life and Glory
558. When the Victory to Gain
559. When There Dawns upon Our World
560. When Weak and Heavy Laden
561. When with the Angels Christ Jesus Shall Come
562. When Your Sky Is Overcast
563. Where Are My Sins Today?

564. While for You God's Children Here Are Praying
565. Whisper the Name of Jesus
566. Who, Ah, Who Is This I See?
567. Who Died to Redeem Me?
568. [Who Shall Be Able to Stand?](#)
569. Who Will Toil for Jesus?
570. Who Your Guilt Can Bear Away?
571. Why Not, O Why Not Decide It Tonight?
572. Wide Fling the Gospel Banner
573. With Aching Heart to God I Cried
574. With Our Eyes on Our Wonderful Savior
575. With the Red Sea Ahead
576. Would You Find an Open Fountain?
577. Would You Lift Some Comrade Dear?
578. Would You Lift Some Weary Comrade?
579. Would You Lose Your Weight of Sadness?
580. Would You the Forces of Evil Restrain?
581. Ye Stricken Souls, This Message Hear
582. Ye Who Are Weary, Hopeless and Dreary?
583. Yielding All to Jesus
584. You May Keep on Working Till Your Life Is O'er
585. You May Keep on Working Till Your Life's Last Hour
586. You May Know This Day
587. You Mean to Be Holy Sometimes
588. You Surely Have Found That the Savior Is Real
589. Your Earthly Race Is Almost Run[139]

---

[139] http://www.hymntime.com/tch/bio/h/a/r/r/i/s/harris_t.htm
- *Canterbury Dictionary of Hymnology*, **accessed 9 Jan 2020**

Chapter 5

ALL THAT THRILLS MY SOUL

If you don't know where you are going, then any road will take you there.

- Bishop Bernie L. Wade

Publishing
Thoro Harris published a plethora of Song Books. Many featured his own songs, and some were compilations with other composers. "He wrote hundreds of Christian songs. He published hundreds of other songs he didn't write. Thoro Harris was one of the most prolific African American hymn writers of the early 20th century. Since the 1930s his compositions have been consistently selected for publication in hymnals of various denominations. We have only highlighted a few in these pages.

Gospel Themes
Thoro's most repeated theme is our relationship with Jesus. The second one is Jesus' second coming. His songs reflect the joy of the believing in living for Jesus Christ. While his songs represent his most heartfelt beliefs they are not generally doctrinally pointed or focused on Christianeze, denominational distinctives or organizational focuses.

More Abundantly (1914)
For a person hearing this song for the first time, the final verse introduces the way into the life that Jesus said He came to give "more abundantly" (John 10:10): "Come to Him believing, Hearken to His call; All from Him receiving, Yield to Him your all; Jesus will accept you When to Him you flee; He will grant His blessing more abundantly."

The first verse asks the listener very directly if they're actually living the abundant life. It tells how to be certain as a believer to live life to the fullest. It says, "Are you trusting Jesus, All along the way? Does He grow more precious To your heart each day? Are you, His disciple? Test His Word and see, He will give the Spirit more abundantly."

He's Coming Soon (1918)
For this song Thoro borrowed the Hawaiian tune "Aloha Oe," written by the beloved Queen Liliuokalani of the Hawaiian people. "It is said that she could play guitar, piano, organ, ukulele and zither, and she sang alto, performing Hawaiian and English sacred and secular music. She wrote almost 165 songs, of which the best known is the extremely popular Aloha Oe — the tune for "He's Coming Soon." Aloha Oe was published around 1890."

In her memoirs, Liliuokalani wrote, "To compose was as natural to me as to breathe, and this gift of nature, never having been suffered to fall into disuse, remains a source of the greatest consolation in composing, and transcribed a number of songs. Three found their way from my prison to the city of Chicago, where they were printed, among them 'Aloha Oe' or 'Farewell to Thee', which became a very popular song."[140] It is likely that these songs coming to the attention of the people of Chicago also captured the attention of Thoro Harris.

The Pacific Island flavor especially helps the chorus that's coupled with Jesus' words (Mark 13:33-15) to remind us of our destination to a land that surpasses anything here on earth:

---

[140] https://www.thedestinlog.com/story/lifestyle/faith/2012/11/09/1-46859/33719898007/

"He's coming soon, He's coming soon; With joy we welcome His returning; It may be morn, it may be night or noon— We know He's coming soon."

The final verse echoes I Thessalonians 4:18: "This hope we cherish not in vain, but we comfort one another by this word."

CHILDREN'S SONGS

Other hymn writers have penned lyrics to songs for children. Not many have three that have survived as strongly as the following songs by Thoro.

Jesus Loves the Little Children 1921)

Without doubt this is the song that has the largest audience. In nearly all Christian denominations, organizations, and more children learn this song. It is a song that speaks to the depth of Thoro Harris. As a man born to a black father and a white mother, caught in a world overtly focused on racial division, it is without doubt that Thoro could reflect on the words of the refrain "red & yellow; black & white".

There are two versions of this song. The first, written shortly before 1900, includes lyrics by C. H. Woolston and a tune by George F. Root. That version begins with the words "Jesus calls the children dear." Its chorus is today's most familiar one: "Jesus loves the little children, All the children of the world. Red, and yellow, black and white, they are precious in His sight. Jesus loves the little children of the world."

Thoro must have felt inspired to write his own version. He and C. H. Woolston are both credited in hymnals in which the songs begin with the line "In the lands beyond the sea Countless million children be." The chorus also differs by stating "Jesus loves the little children, All the children of the world. Little ones are His delight, they are precious in His sight. Jesus loves the little children of the world."

I Love Him Better Every Day (1926)
The chorus concludes with, "Close by His side, I will abide. I love Him better every day." I've always heard it sung by spelling out the last word of each line in the chorus, so that the entire chorus says, "I love Him better every d-a-y. I love Him better every d-a-y. Close by His s-i-d-e, I will a-b-i-d-e. I love Him better every d-a-y. " Thoro wrote the verses and Major Sydney Cox of the Salvation Army added the refrain.[141]

Grumblers (1929)
Verse, one says, "In country town or city, Some people can be found, Who spend their lives in grumbling at everything around. Oh yes, they always grumble, No matter what you say, For these are chronic grumblers, And they grumble night and day."

The chorus follows with "Oh, they grumble on Monday, Tuesday, Wednesday Grumble on Thursday to; Grumble on Friday, Saturday, Sunday, Grumble the whole week through."

---

[141] https://kenschristiandevotions.com/2024/05/14/sidney-e-cox/

The remaining verses describe where people grumble, to whom, and about what.

Peter Phillip Bilhorn

A Christian musician named Peter Phillip Bilhorn invited Thoro to Chicago, Illinois. Bilhorn's family name was originally Pulhorn; it was changed by a judge in Ottawa, Illinois, named **Abraham Lincoln.** Peter and his brother formed the Eureka Wagon and Carriage Works in Chicago, Illinois. Later, Peter became involved in Gospel music, studying under **George Root, George Stebbins**, and others. He wrote some 2,000 Gospel songs in his lifetime, and for a while, worked with evangelist **Billy Sunday**. He also invented a folding pump organ used at revivals in the late 19th Century, and founded the *Bilhorn Folding Organ Company*[142] in Chicago, Illinois. One of the high points in Bilhorn's career came in 1900, when he traveled to London. There he conducted a 4,000 strong choir in the Crystal Palace, and Queen Victoria invited him to sing in Buckingham Palace.

In the windy city, Thoro took a job as an editor at the Glad Tidings Publishing Company,[143] promoting the songs of many other hymn writers through the songbooks he edited. One of his collaborations was adding music to L. B. Tolbert's words for "Hide Thou Me."

Hide Thou Me (1926)

---

[142] https://antiquitymusic.com/brand/bilhorn.html
[143] The company ceased operations sometime in the 1920s, perhaps in the tumult of the Great Depression.

The song's slow, moving tempo sounds more like African American songs of the 1920s and 1930s, like those of **Thomas Dorsey** and others. Thoro's music fits the lyrics. Verse one: "Sometimes I feel discouraged and think my life in vain. I'm tempted then to murmur, and of my lot complain; But when I think of Jesus, and all He's done for me, Then I cry, O Rock of Ages, hide Thou me."

Thoro Harris

From the early 1930s until his death in 1955, Thoro lived in Eureka Springs, Arkansas. Here's his most well-known song from that period.

All That Thrills My Soul is Jesus (1931) This hymn has survived with strength beyond any of Thoro's other songs. The chorus boldly proclaims "All that thrills my soul is Jesus; He is more than life to me. And the fairest of ten thousand, In my blessed Lord I see." The song speaks volumes about how Thoro Harris interpreted Scripture, Christian living and the relationship with Jesus Christ.

The verses mention reasons for living a Christ-centered life. Key phrases are "Who can cheer the heart like Jesus, By His presence all divine?" "Love of Christ so freely given, Grace of God beyond degree," and "Ev'ry need His hand supplying."

Gospel Quintet Songs

A rare edition of this African American songbook previously published with fewer songs by the same compiler in Chicago; this edition was printed in Eureka Springs, Arkansas. The five men are part of **The Cleveland Colored Quintet.**[144]

From left to right: Floyd H. Lacy, J. W. Parker, Spurgeon Jones, H. D. Hodges, and Alexander Talbert

Representing the finest in gospel music, the members of the Cleveland Gospel Quintet were, in their own words, brought by God "in a mysterious way from different parts  of the U.S.A. to Cleveland, Ohio, where they were saved one by one through the efforts of The Christian and Missionary Alliance."

[144144] https://cmalliance.org/the-cleveland-gospel-quintet/

They began singing as a quartet in 1913. Needing another tenor, they prayed for the salvation of Floyd H. Lacy, who was then singing with the popular Musical Magpies.[145] God answered. Lacy joined, and the group became a quintet.[146]

Thoro also produced a book for a less mainstream group. In 1943 he worked in collaboration with **Rev. Floyd Humble** of Chicago, IL to produce **Songs of Summerland** published in Eureka Springs, AK. How connected Harris was with the group remains uncertain. It seems he first made the connection with a local group of Spiritualist in the Eureka Springs area (perhaps that was Humble). Humble is notorious as a leader in the Spiritualist movement and later (1967) founded the **United Spiritualist Church**.[147]

Those who knew him said that Thoro Harris was known to carry around a bag of his songbooks wherever he went. He lived the final twenty-plus years of his life in Eureka Springs, moving there in 1932 and passing away there in 1955.

---

[145] https://www.amazon.sg/Musical-Magpies-Story-Thomas-Elwood/dp/1952905001
[146] https://cmalliance.org/the-cleveland-gospel-quintet/
[147] https://www.encyclopedia.com/science/encyclopedias-almanacs-transcripts-and-maps/united-spiritualist-church

Thoro Harris died on March 27, 1955, in Eureka Springs, Ark. He was 80 years old.[148] He was buried at the International Order of Odd Fellows Cemetery, Eureka Springs Carroll County, Arkansas, USA

His last words, *"The Light is almost over"*.

---

[148] https://ffbosworth.mystrikingly.com/blog/f-f-bosworth-and-thoro-harris-a-moment-in-black-history

Bernie L. Wade, Sr., PhD serves the International Circle of Faith (ICOF) as Presiding Bishop. This global, multiracial, multi-cultural, nondenominational fellowship has over 40,000 active ministers and is considered one of the largest apostolic groups in history. Wade is also the President of the Christian World Network www.christianworldnet.com Wade holds 4 earned doctorates and serves as Chancellor for Life College & Seminary. www.lifecollege.education

Bernie L. Wade, PhD
Chancellor

For more information or copies of these books contact:
Bernie L. Wade 6321 Fallen Timber Road Sulphur, Kentucky 40070   Bernie.wade1212@gmail.com

Other books by Bishop Bernie L. Wade, PhD:

Made in the USA
Middletown, DE
04 February 2025